DESIGNING JAPAN

DESIGNING JAPAN

JAPAN

A FUTURE BUILT ON AESTHETICS

KENYA HARA

TRANSLATED BY MAGGIE KINSER HOHLE AND YUKIKO NAITO

Note on Japanese Romanization

A modified Hepburn system of romanization is used for Japanese terms, including the names of people and places, that omits diacritical marks such as macrons and apostrophes. Long vowels are not indicated by macrons. The spelling of non-Japanese words that have been incorporated into Japanese reflects the way these words are pronounced by Japanese speakers. For Japanese names, we are following the convention of using the Western order for the names of modern and contemporary Japanese and the traditional order for historical figures (family name first, followed by the personal name).

Designing Japan: A Future Built on Aesthetics
by Kenya Hara. Translated by Maggie Kinser Hohle and Yukiko Naito.

Published by
Japan Publishing Industry Foundation for Culture (JPIC)
3-12-3 Kanda-Jinbocho, Chiyoda-ku, Tokyo 101-0051, Japan

First English edition: March 2018

This book is a translation of *Nihon no dezain: Biishiki ga tsukuru mirai* (Iwanami Shoten, 2011). English publishing rights arranged with Iwanami Shoten, Publishers, Tokyo.

Book design: Kenya Hara + Sebastian Fehr
Hara Design Institute, Nippon Design Center, Inc.

As this book is published primarily to be donated to overseas universities, research institutions, public libraries and other organizations, commercial publication rights are available. For all enquiries regarding those rights, please contact the publisher of the English edition at the following address: japanlibrary@jpic.or.jp

Printed in Japan
ISBN 978-4-86658-015-9
http://www.jpic.or.jp/japanlibrary/

Contents

Preface to the English Edition

Japan, an archipelago that extends in an arc off the northeastern coast of the Eurasian continent, has the rare history of having been an independent nation throughout its history. Originally an agricultural country that centered on rice cultivation, Japan has thrived on industry since World War II, more than seventy years. Because Japan has limited natural resources, the nation's economy has been built on manufacturing products for export using imported raw materials. Accordingly, the entire nation has been utilized as a vast manufacturing facility. Our coastlines were shackled with concrete blockades and lined with petrochemical complexes from which we exported industrial products to the rest of the world. Densely populated cities were linked by high-speed railroads and expressways, the latter becoming congested with cars. Having sustained intense economic growth for some time, we then experienced the collapse of a bubble economy and began to shift toward a postindustrial society. Today we face complex social problems, including a dwindling birth rate and an aging population, with multifaceted consequences.

Let us consider the resources we do have. Much of our land is covered in mountain greenery. The country is rich in water flowing from the mountains, and the seasonal changes are exquisitely subtle. Seas surround our islands, the land is rich in hot springs, and our traditional cuisine revolves around the four distinct seasons. Above all we can benefit from an immense accumulation of culture and the aesthetics nurtured over thousands of years. Now is the time for us to firmly identify and make full use of these values, fused with technology, as *future resources*.

This book is not intended only for Japanese readers. Fundamentally, global and local are a dyad. The essence of culture is locality itself; there is no global culture. With the growth of international fluidity, local brilliance enriches the whole world; focusing on the values of our own countries surely contributes to this global abundance. This volume suggests a path for Japan to move toward this new horizon.

The original title for this series of essays was "The Education of Desire." If objects are created in response to human desires, the quality of those desires drives the quality of products and services, and of society itself. If humankind has wisdom, our future happiness rests entirely on how we can educate our desires. Design is a gentle education that influences the quality of desire. This is both an issue for today's Japan and a shared issue for the whole world. I hope that this book, translated into English, can present a collective opportunity for even more people to consider this way of thinking. I will be happy if through the medium of this volume, people who had not thought at all about Japan will begin to imagine a future for the world that builds on ideas from this island nation.

Preface

Japan is at a turning point in its history. Since the end of World War II, we have forged ahead with industrial production, reveling in economic development. But today, with the emergence of other Asian economies, the end is near for the simple economic model of Japan as an industrial nation; we need a plan for re-establishing our nation on a new foundation. At the same time, a declining birth rate and an aging population confront us with unprecedented social and economic circumstances. We are also beginning to see rapid change in patterns of energy production and consumption and a new quest for innovative ways of thinking about agriculture and tourism.

Every Japanese citizen must sense this critical juncture, and faintly yet steadily, a question is arising, one that has been continually suppressed since the Meiji Restoration in 1868, when we began to steer our economy and culture toward Westernization: Would the potential and pride of our nation not be better served by restoring a sensibility cultivated over thousands of years rather than allowing it to continue to be diluted?

I once wrote that the essence of design is "the education of desire." Products and environments are harvests reaped from the soil of human desire. To create quality products and environments, we have to actualize well-fertilized soil by refining human desire. Design is fundamental to the process. Interacting with well-thought-out design induces an awakening, from which changes in our desires arise, resulting in modifications to patterns of consumption, resource utilization, and finally, lifestyle. From the soil of fertile and healthy desires comes fruit – products and environments – of superior quality.

If the term "desire" sounds too raw, we might replace it with "aspiration," but to express the power of a certain longing, the former seems more fitting. And I deliberately chose the word "education" because in addition to the perspective of instruction, it implies bringing potential to fruition.

At any rate, we mustn't allow desire to become willful and self-indulgent. Marketing likes to talk about "needs," but needs can tend toward the loose and slovenly. It will not do to cultivate desires as undisciplined needs. Culture and aesthetics provide guidance and boundaries. And it is here that design must play an active role.

This book speaks to the future of Japan rather than reviewing its past. Design is an intention toward a desired end; its role is to imagine and plan the form of that end. The essence of design is to make visible underlying potential and reveal an explicit, significant path for the future, to clearly delineate a vision that can be shared with many. The turning point we face has acquired even greater significance in light of the formidable impact of the 2011 Tohoku earthquake. This reinforced my intention to write a book from a practical perspective based on personal experience, concerning the future of fabrication and manufacturing, the hospitality and tourism industry, and a society with an aging population and declining birth rate.

I identify many of these areas as fields to which I will devote myself as a designer.

In the preface to my 2014 book *Designing Design*, I wrote, "Verbalizing design is another act of design." I remain committed to this view. However, with this book, I would like to move on to the work of imagining and planning the future.

These are the themes I wish to address here.

Introduction: Aesthetics as a Resource

Introduction: Aesthetics as a Resource

Whenever I get off a flight at Narita Airport and pass through that impersonal space, walking toward passport control, I have the same feeling. While it is boring and lifeless, I can't help but admire how scrupulously clean and well kept it is. All the floor tiles gleam; it makes you think that you could roll on them without even dirtying your clothes. The carpet is immaculate too. You see traces of the best efforts to remove even minor stains. I am certain that the cleaners who work here never put away their mops and vacuums the minute their shift ends; they continue until they complete a task. Returning from another country, I'm always keenly aware of their attentiveness, their consideration. Even as I leave the airport in a car on the expressway, this feeling endures. I take no pleasure in the denatured scenery, but the road surface is as smooth as a mirror, the car's engine is quiet, and not a single streetlight illuminating the route is burnt out.

This impression soon merges into the nightscape of the city center, its intricacy and complexity stimulating my senses. Each of the innumerable lights shines steadily and reliably; not one flickers or is out. Combined, they become high-rises extending into the distance as an immense accumulation of light.

The nightscape of contemporary Tokyo may be the most beautiful in the world. Some might object, saying that Tokyo is no match for the view at night of Mumbai or Hong Kong seen from Victoria Peak. People will inevitably have their own preferences; those who agree with mine are surprisingly few. Yet just when I was beginning to doubt myself, I happened to see a TV documentary about cities that quoted international airline pilots as agreeing that right now, the most beautiful nightscape in the world is Tokyo's. These experts should know. Naturally I approved. Though the world is vast, there is no other city with Tokyo's expansive reach – the sheer scale at which all those lights are concentrated.

Whether cleaning, building, cooking, or maintaining good lighting, Japanese generally do their jobs carefully and conscientiously. If we were to put the values underlying them into specific words, we could say they have "delicacy," "thoroughness," "precision," and "simplicity." Japan is a country guided by these values.

The same values are not easily found overseas. For instance, if you wanted to produce an exhibition venue with the attention to detail found in Japan – whether in Paris, Milan, or London – it would take an unusual effort. Fundamentally, the same diligence is lacking. At quitting time, laborers stop working. The sanctity of individuals insisting on doing things their own way and at their own pace overrides the desire to perfect the quality and efficiency of the work. So management controls the process with a light hand. Certainly in Europe there exists a spirit of craftsmanship. However, I doubt that it extends into the realm of routine cleaning or the construction of exhibition venues. To go further, I have a feeling that the mindfulness involved in preparing an ordinary, everyday environment is not only an issue for those doing the work, but also is connected to the level of consciousness of the general public sharing that environment. We don't leave a lofty consciousness to the special domain of the craftsman alone; to neatly maintain mundane, everyday spaces is an example of the common sense and courtesy that is tacitly shared throughout Japanese society. And aesthetics, I believe, are what underlie this kind of behavior.

Lately, I have begun to think that aesthetics is precisely the resource needed for making things. This is in no way a metaphor. An object is conceived and nurtured only within a culture in which the shared sensitivity of the creator and the admirer of the object is recognized and appreciated. Truly, aesthetics is the perpetual resource that allows the creation of things, the artistry, to continue. However, most people attach a different sense to "resource," usually seeing it only in terms of natural resources.

It is a common assumption that Japan developed sophisticated technologies for the production of industrial goods because it is not blessed with natural resources, and that rapid economic growth following World War II was an achievement born of the pursuit of manufacturing under this scheme. The world at large and the Japanese themselves share this perception. The industrial production at which postwar Japan excelled was standardized mass production: manufacturing large volumes of goods uniformly to exceptionally stable tolerances. Then, by applying our ability to miniaturize products, we succeeded in clearly establishing the superiority of Japanese industrial goods. Our industrial technology has earned a reputation globally as a result of quality premised on quantity, as well as the precision and compactness of its products.

However, the technology of which we speak here is the ability to perform manufacturing tasks "delicately," "thoroughly," "precisely," and "simply" – the refinement of skills acquired through the appropriate application of the "resource of sensibility." My contention is that the same sensibility behind the immaculately polished airport floor and the fact that all the city's lights can be counted on to function might also be at work in standardized mass production. In this lies the basis of the idea that the resource that creates sophisticated manufacturing technology is in fact an aesthetic consciousness.

Japan lacks natural resources like oil and iron ore. This is a fact that greatly influenced national policy during a critical phase of history, and was one of the primary factors that plunged us into World War II. Now, however, our focus on natural resource security may be turning into an asset. If oil gushed from the earth in Japan, our awareness of the environment and energy conservation would not have grown as it has. And with oil and gas, this glorious natural habitat, mountainous and surrounded by the sea, might have been spoiled and polluted to the point of no return, and we might not have taken the initiative to chair an international conference in Kyoto on regulating the greenhouse gas emissions causing climate change. Or we might have been faced with a situation in which China and the United States were urgently trying to persuade Japan to curb its carbon dioxide emissions and oil consumption. Or we might have become a country that accumulated great reserves of monetary wealth, an affluent nation able to provide everything – medical services, education, telecommunications – free of charge. Yet in the end, that affluence, unable to adapt to the future, might eventually have led to a disastrous decline.

Fortunately, Japan has almost no natural resources. The resource that has made our nation prosper lies in another dimension. I refer to the wisdom and the sensibility behind organizing an environment with delicacy, thoroughness, precision, and simplicity. Natural resources can be purchased as long as their global circulation is secure. Money buys Australian aluminum or Russian oil. But the "resource of sensibility," long nurtured at the root of culture, can't be bought. This valuable resource can't be exported, even if it's in demand.

Japan's industrial products have already begun to demonstrate their superiority from the perspectives of moderation and energy consumption, and their sophistication in response to the maturity of the users. The fact that Japanese auto manufacturers at one time recorded the highest sales in the world offers a partial explanation of this phenomenon, although it has been easy to overlook in the context of the global recession. Ordinary people have also begun to respond positively to energy conservation and the need to alleviate the burden on the environment, sustaining in their daily lives the inclination and the good sense to avoid excess and practice moderation.

What if we were to re-examine how our own culture might contribute, from the resources of our sensibilities, to the rest of the world? By so doing, we would be able to face the future knowing our country is one that can present in a balanced way traits that the world will inevitably need going forward: restraint and rationality.

We are facing an era in which industrial technology is spreading throughout Asia and elsewhere. This is no time to lament the deindustrialization of our own country. We have to consider decisively shifting the center of gravity in production from quantity to quality. We need to focus not only on industrial production but also on our rich natural environment by applying our aesthetic resources to the service and hospitality sectors. By doing so, I believe that Japan could establish a presence as a new type of environmentally oriented country capable of making the most of nature from both a practical and aesthetic point of view. While there are no oil wells here, hot springs abound. We should be able to stand on the stage of a new economic culture harnessing aesthetics as a resource, applying this to residential and office environments, refinement of the fields of mobility and communication, compassion in medical care and social welfare, and comfort at hotels and resorts.

Let's accept as a given fact the rise of China and India. It's Asia's time. Since the era of Japan's high economic growth, we have come to pride ourselves on our GDP, but it seems time now to escape that spell. I would like Japan, in ceding large GDPs to more populous countries, to look much further ahead, while paying close attention to the present. From our position on the extreme eastern edge of Asia, we should aim for the height of sophistication, attained only after having undergone deep contact and friction with other cultures.

At the vanguard of growth, whether in technology, life, or art, there function sensibilities imperceptibly attuned to, and capable of deftly perceiving, the world and the future. Look there. The world is enriched only when we vie with one another in this aesthetic arena.

Chapter 1

Movement: A Design Platform

Confronting a Crowded World

Japan is an industrialized country, a major exporter of goods to the world, but we rarely think or talk about whether these products can be said to nurture any kind of culture. Culture is not rooted in the arts alone; ascertaining and offering the kind of lifestyle or activities associated with certain products, or the kind of environment the products foster, influences the future of the world. In the future, competition will not be over the power of money but over the power to influence that accompanies culture. Clout is not measured simply in total product output or the size of the GDP. Japan has to have the will and take the responsibility to exemplify a convincing presence not only in economic terms, but also in terms of imagining how people can live richer lives – and for that, it is essential to bring a multilateral enquiry and vision to the cultural meaning of the things we make.

But we'll be too late if we wait for government and industry to slowly recognize this and put their backs into it with this perspective. Wanting to put our thoughts into action, the architect Shigeru Ban and I established a small nonprofit organization called Design Platform Japan to launch an exhibition introducing Japan's industrial culture from a design viewpoint to overseas audiences. We began to work together during our spare time, using our offices and staff.

The result was *JAPAN CAR: Designs for the Crowded Globe*, an exhibition held at science museums in London and Paris from November 2008 to April 2009. It was achieved with the participation of seven automobile manufacturers, a company that creates the large-scale technology that underpins our social infrastructure, and a firm specializing in interaction technologies, all from Japan. Mr. Ban was in charge of its composition, and I supervised curation and graphic design.

At one point, I asked Ban why he was doing all this free of charge. He answered immediately, "It's out of a sense of mission." In that straightforward reply was something that moved me. As long as we are involved in architecture and design, it would be useless, and perhaps not even fulfill our professional obligations, if we didn't participate in the process of harvesting our work in association with culture.

Ban is an architect who has gained more attention abroad than in Japan for his work utilizing cardboard tubes as a building material. Currently he is based in Paris. At first glance, the tubes seem weak, but as an architectural material they possess special properties: adequate strength and ease of production as well as post-demolition recycling. The ingenuity he has focused on this material and the many architectural uses to which he has put it have attracted the interest and admiration of others in the field. In 2010, the Centre Pompidou-Metz was completed in northeastern France following a design on which Ban collaborated with the French architect Jean de Gastines.

Ban and I are the same age. At the time of the *JAPAN CAR* exhibition, we were fifty, but we weren't particularly close. We have developed a working relationship bit by bit, as I, with my interest in his work, invited him to participate in various design-themed exhibitions I curated, such as *RE DESIGN: Daily Products of the 21st Century* and *HAPTIC: Awakening the Senses*. Ban is a daring creator with the courage to build architecture out of paper and the energy to break through convention. As for me, I am a graphic designer who makes experiences rather than things, specializing in broadcasting the seeds of images, memory, understanding, and identity. So even if we might be said to have different professional styles and attributes, we can work together in a complementary manner.

The genesis of our close working relationship was an announcement by fashion designer Issey Miyake in the *Asahi Shimbun* in January 2003, calling for the creation of a design museum in Japan. The gist of the proposal was that it was disgraceful that while Japan had become an international leader in manufacturing, there was no design museum here in which the nation's industrial achievements could be exhibited in light of their cultural significance.

Ban quickly endorsed the proposal and conceived the idea of building the museum as an annex to a proposed casino resort on the artificial island of Odaiba in Tokyo Bay. When he was making arrangements to present this plan to Shintaro Ishihara, the governor of Tokyo, Ban came to consult me. A certain magazine had decided to devote an entire issue to Ban's plan, and he wanted me to collaborate in developing it.

I designed a logo as if the museum already existed and, imagining the first exhibition, made a poster and tickets for it. I then took photos for the magazine: downtown scenes in which

Signage from a series of simulated images created for the article "Tokyo's Design Museum Concept: Why Is There No Design Museum in Tokyo?" *Dream Design* 11 (2003)

the poster appeared plastered here and there, realistic shots of used admission tickets damp with rain on the stairs of a footbridge, and scenes of people walking about wearing T-shirts bearing the exhibition logo. I also made packing tape with the museum logo for the museum gift shop, roughing out the idea that this new product could be used to recycle ordinary shopping bags into museum bags. I photographed street scenes in which people holding the bags stood at bus stops and elsewhere. Directional signage was printed on tall stacks of containers with the logo and arrows boldly rendered in white. This series of simulated images, presented as a magazine article, really did make it seem as if the museum was already up and running. The special issue, including Ban's complete architectural plan and the management plan for the museum, was published in November 2003.

In the end, Governor Ishihara didn't show much interest in the project, and the proposal was not accepted. At the time, we had imagined that the first show would be "Unbuilt Architecture" – an exhibition of unrealized proposals. Thinking back on it now, I see the irony. But we were not terribly discouraged. Architecture and design are mostly a series of competitions, so we didn't lose heart. Even if you don't win a competition, the ideas that result from the effort accumulate in your idea bank. As they accrue, your creative energy gains strength. The hypothetical museum ended as a concept, but through the simulation experience, the pressure of wanting to realize it mounted.

Before long, hoping to build some momentum for this project, we contacted automobile manufacturers Toyota, Nissan, and Honda, and heads of the design departments of high-tech companies such as Sony Creative Center, Panasonic, and Hitachi, and convened a symposium about the creation of a design museum at the Maison Franco-Japonaise in Tokyo in 2005. Speakers included the contemporary art curator Kazuko Koike, the architectural historian Riichi Miyake, and the architect Kengo Kuma. Professional opinions were exchanged concerning corporate perspectives on design and culture. But, in light of the practical problems involved in collecting and managing a great number of products, as well as the enormous amount of space, equipment, and labor this would entail, interest in establishing a large-scale public institution gradually faded. On the other hand, a consensus was reached that we needed a multilateral platform through which to compile design information, and this turned out to be the result of the conference. Naturally, if your aim is a big-box museum, the building budget and management costs all swell enormously – but if you are interested purely in a "planning engine" that functions as a way of gathering and exchanging related information, it requires neither a physical facility nor a collection.

This is how the idea surfaced for a "design platform" rather than a museum. For several years after that, Ban and I slowly brought our concept closer to fruition. We planned and implemented an exhibition with industry and design in Japan as the theme, and toured it internationally. Our attitude was that if we could do that, then we knew where we should initially focus our energy.

JAPAN CAR: Designs for the Crowded Globe was the first exhibition conceived under these circumstances. We chose cars because we thought it was essential to begin with a challenging subject. In Japan, where the automobile industry prospers, there are eight major manufacturers of passenger vehicles, every one of which is like a goshawk on the forest canopy of the ecosystem we call industry. It was unlikely that any one of these companies would be open to our opinions, but if we were able to work with them to create a single message, it would be a groundbreaking event and might attract international interest. To put it another way, if we could implement an idea of that scale, we could do anything.

From symposium to exhibition took three years. We didn't move at a leisurely pace by any means. Ban and I had fewer opportunities for meetings than we had expected, but it was also because people were not optimistic enough about our ability to actualize this kind of proposal. Despite diligently explaining ourselves to the Automobile Division of the Ministry of Economy, Trade and Industry (METI) and working assiduously on the Japanese Automobile Manufacturers Association, nothing budged. However, after we wrote countless letters to the design departments of the car manufacturers that had gathered at the symposium, rewrote our proposal multiple times, applied a lot of persuasion and had many meetings to convince them, the heavy gate swung open a little.

JAPAN CAR Exhibition

Take a dispassionate look at the cars on the road today. Lately, we've seen a clear trend in Japanese production. You'll recognize it soon enough if you pay just a little attention: there's been a marked drop in the number of luxury sedans and sporty coupes that formed the mainstream until just recently, while boxy compact cars have multiplied; the proportion of cars designed with a focus on practicality has risen sharply.

Over time, the infatuation with style and status has declined in favor of something more utilitarian. More and more, the car is being treated as a daily necessity – simple to enter and exit, convenient for carrying things. This is also why fuel-efficient hybrid cars are popular. Navigation systems, automatic toll-collection systems, and the like – once specially installed options – are now offered by the manufacturer, and are playing a part in less wasteful driving and relief of traffic congestion. The fading perception of the car as a compelling way to express one's fashion sense or lifestyle is probably why young people today have no particular interest in having a car.

The car has already become an ordinary everyday tool. Accordingly, the objectives are function and efficiency, and designs that embody these – with neither too much, nor too little – have come to dominate. It's difficult to say whether we should see this tendency as bleak or as an indication of maturity and a proper understanding of objects. What is important is that, in Japanese car design, an originality not found in other cultural realms has emerged. The exhibition, aiming to distill, pinpoint, and introduce the distinctive traits of today's Japanese cars as well as how these traits can contribute to today's world, drew large audiences and won critical acclaim. It was arranged around three perspectives: compactness, environmental technology, and mobile urban cells. These themes are worth examining further.

As preparations for the exhibition got into full swing and we met with the people in the design departments of Toyota, Nissan, and Honda, we unexpectedly discovered a consensus on the unique features of today's Japanese cars. The representatives of all three companies singled out Daihatsu's Tanto. What is distinctive about this vehicle is that it's a pretty straightforward square, making full use of the specifications for length, width, and height of a *kei*, or light passenger, car. European cars are designed to reduce aerodynamic resistance, so every surface, including the front windshield, is inclined diagonally. Naturally, with the low interior ceiling, people have to stoop to get in. In Europe, there seems to be an implicit and deep-seated view that cars that don't look fast are losers, having abandoned agility and the desire for speed. The Tanto, however, relinquishes streamlining and instead prioritizes comfort and livability.

Because its structure is stable enough without a central pillar, standard in most cars, it has none, making it very easy to get in. Boarding is made comfortable by the fact that the car is two meters high and the back door is vertical and slides wide open horizontally like a shoji screen. In addition, the floor is completely flat. There is certainly less of a sense of speed and

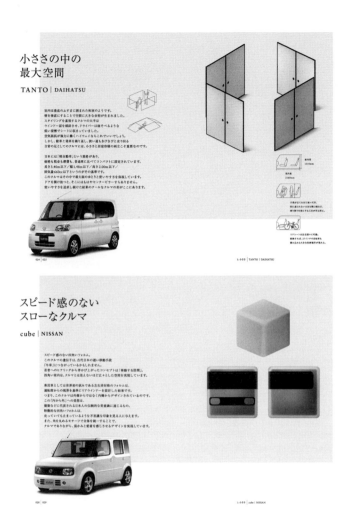

小ささの中の
最大空間

TANTO | DAIHATSU

室内は畳廊のふすまに囲まれた和室のようです。
壁を垂直にすることで空間に大きな余裕が生まれました。
スタイリングを重視するクルマの大半は
ウインドー面を傾斜させ、ドライバーは寝そべるような
低い姿勢でシートに収まっていました。
空気抵抗が抑えに働く「ハイウェイ」ならこれでいいでしょう。
しかし、発着と発車を繰り返し、使い道もきびきびと走り回る
日常の足としてのクルマには、小ささと居住容積の両立こそ重要なのです。

日本には「軽自動車」という規格があり、
価格も税金も優遇し、普通車に比べてコンパクトに設定されています。
長さ3.40m以下／幅1.48m以下／高さ2.00m以下
排気量660cc以下というのがその基準です。
このクルマはその中で最大限の余ゆとりと使いやすさを実現しています。
ドアを開け放つと、そこにはもはやセンターピラーすらありません。
使いやすさを追求し続けた結果のクールなクルマの形がここにあります。

スピード感のない
スローなクルマ

cube | NISSAN

スピード感のない四角いフォルム。
このクルマの遺伝子は、古代日本の遅い移動手段
「牛車」につながっているかもしれません。
若者へのヒアリングから浮かび上がったコンセプトは「移動する閉間」。
四角い室内は、クルマとは思えないほど広々とした空間を実現しています。

乗用車としては世界初の試みである左右非対称のフォルムは、
運転席からの視界を基準にデザインした結果です。
つまり、このクルマは外側からではなく「内側からデザインされている」のです。
建築などに代表される日本人の伝統的な美意識に通じるもの。
窓枠的な四角いフォルムは。
走っていても止まっているような不思議な印象を見る人に与えます。
また、角を丸めるモチーフで全体を統一することで、
クルマでありながら、温かみと愛着を感じさせるデザインを実現しています。

Above: Daihatsu Tanto
Below: Nissan Cube

masculinity, but this is made up for by its obvious appeal as a tool for daily life.

There are many small cars in the world. The cobbled streets of Europe can be as narrow as Japan's roads, so plenty of cars are small in scale. Around Italy, you see countless tiny unlicensed vehicles driven by students and such. Lately, the two-person Mercedes-Benz Smart has also become popular. However, all of these utilize an aerodynamic body, as nimble as a sneaker; you won't come across any square cars in Europe.

In Japan, there are official regulations defining *kei* cars. They must be no more than 3.4 meters long, 1.48 meters wide, 2 meters high, and have an engine displacement no greater than 660 cubic centimeters. Thanks to benefits like low taxes and exemption from parking space certification, more than one in three cars in Japan is now a *kei* car. This is not because the streets are especially narrow or because Japanese people aren't tall. The goal of the design was economic rationality. Many years dedicated to making full use of these specifications have borne fruit: a square format that is not simply small, but represents a concentration of knowledge and technology. Nissan's Cube is not a *kei* car but derives from the same "square car" design philosophy. It seems likely that in future this will be one of the shapes that will be recognized around the world as representative of Japanese car design.

Toyota's iQ embodies an even more novel compactness. It is the same width as an ordinary four-seater, with spacious driver and passenger seats, but is much shorter than a standard *kei*: less

世界最小
4人乗りプレミアムカー

iQ | TOYOTA

車幅は小型乗用車サイズにもかかわらず、
全長は「軽」の基準よりもさらに短く3m未満の超小型サイズ。
この独自のボリュームが大胆でアイコニックなデザインに流されています。
超高効率なパッケージは、燃費効率にも直結し、CO₂の排出量は99g／km（欧州仕様）。
小さいけれども乗り心地や動力性能はトップクラスへ。
まさにプレミアムクラスの小型車です。
衝突安全性は、欧州の安全基準
EURO NCAPにて5つ星を獲得しています。
エアバッグは9カ所に装備されています。
最小回転半径3.9mは、4人乗りのクルマとしては大変小さな数値です。

床席のレイアウトにも特徴があります。
コンポーネントユニットの小型化により、
助手席廻りを大きく小さくなったインパネは、
助手席と後部座席の足長に充分な余地のスペースをもたらしています。
小さいからこそ高機能という日本の知恵が凝縮したクルマです。

3.9m

軽快な小回りが特徴の一つ。
各所の部品やその配置の応用で、
タイヤをより大きく据ることが可能になり、
快敵な機動性が生み出された。

1・小さき | iQ | TOYOTA

超一流の悪路走破性

Jimny | SUZUKI

悪路やオフロードを走破することが目的で作られたクルマですが、
その悪路は強力なパワーだけではありません。
むしろ、軽くてきいことが、悪路走破性の最大の根拠となっています。
大排気量の大型4WDが入り込めないような場所にも機能に入り込める性能は、
軽量・コンパクトというコンセプトから導き出されています。
軽快な運動性は、街中での乗り回しの良さにもつながり、
都市と格外をつなぐ足としても親まれています。
タイヤは4駆でも超小回転します。
小さな体に宿した足回りのたくましさが、その性能を象徴しています。
生活の幅を広く得る、趣味や移道にあわす。
無駄を省いて合理的にクルマを選ぶようになった
ユーザーの成熟にも応えています。

1・小さき | Jimny | SUZUKI

Above: Toyota iQ
Below: Suzuki Jimny

than three meters. Two iQs can fit in one standard parking space. Its minimum turning radius, 3.9 meters, beats even that of the Smart.

Suzuki's Jimny 4WD also shows originality in using its small size to advantage. Its exceptional rough-road capability is the result of a highly refined combination of the power of four-wheel drive and lightweight, compact design. I remember the product designer Naoto Fukasawa calling it "cute" when he got in, and he's right – cute it is, as well as audaciously powerful.

Mazda's Roadster is in the *Guinness Book of World Records* as the world's bestselling two-seater sports car. It's not square, but its lack of expression, created with the cool, detached look of a Noh mask in mind, has earned passionate allegiance.

There was one car that none of the manufacturers were willing to exhibit, the only one that we ourselves bought and brought to the exhibition. That is the *keitora*, or light truck. Able to run along the ridges between rice fields, dart through narrow alleyways, duck under grape arbors, and carry things right up to farmhouse entrances, this vehicle typifies, like a pair of sandals, a thoroughly sensible lifestyle. Its bed is designed for efficient transportation of everything from boxes of apples or mandarin oranges to tatami mats and crates of beer. There is also a surprising variety of cargo platforms for dump trucks and refrigerated vehicles. Japan should certainly be proud of the *kei* truck; it is our transportation intelligence in solid form, a clever compactness that a world tired of excess will surely begin to desire.

The electric cars, hybrid cars, and hydrogen fuel-cell cars

世界で最も多く生産された
二人乗りスポーツ車

ROADSTER | MAZDA

コンパクトに
進化したトラック

HIJET | DAIHATSU

Above: Mazda Roadster
Below: Daihatsu HiJET, a typical kei truck

in the *JAPAN CAR* collection are already being mass produced. One of the fruits of this exhibition was a clear demonstration of this fact. Mitsubishi's electric i-MiEV will run 160 kilometers with one night's charge on household power. That's not quite enough to drive nonstop from Tokyo to Nagoya, but it poses no problem for everyday shopping or getting around town. Toyota's hybrid Prius has already sold more than two million units around the world, and today is the bestselling car in Japan too. When I catch a taxi in Milan, very often it's a Prius, so we can assume that trust in this car has spread internationally.

The Honda FCX Clarity is powered by a hydrogen fuel cell. We tend to think of hydrogen gas as a technology divorced from everyday life, but since 2000 Honda has been developing a hydrogen supply station in southern California that uses solar power to produce hydrogen by water electrolysis. It has been leasing the FCX Clarity there since 2008, and is now ready to mass-produce it. It is the automobile industry that is directly committed to the goal of halving the 1990 level of carbon dioxide emissions by 2050, and the cars in this collection already use the technology that can contribute to reaching it.

We chose fourteen cars that epitomize smart compactness and implement ecological conservation practices, shipped them to Europe with the cooperation of each company, and gathered them at science museums. There was one aspect of this exhibit that we solved ingeniously: we chose white as the uniform color for the cars. Unlike an auto show, the exhibition did not aim to highlight the individual personalities or idiosyncrasies of each

一晩の充電で160km

i-MiEV | MITSUBISHI MOTORS

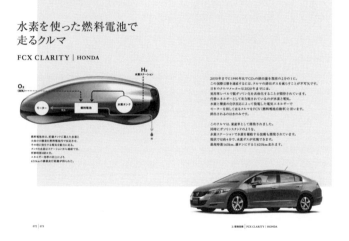

水素を使った燃料電池で
走るクルマ

FCX CLARITY | HONDA

Above: Mitsubishi Motors i-MiEV
Below: Honda FCX Clarity

car to evoke desire for a product. Instead, we wanted the audience to face each automobile – and the thinking behind it – dispassionately. Several colors were considered, but we chose white to disassociate the cars from color.

The first room of the exhibition featured pairings of bonsai and small-scale stylized models of the cars on exhibit. Bonsai symbolizes the bond between humankind and nature; it also demonstrates a refined technique that creates miniature trees and landscapes. Specimens of the highest quality were selected by Seiji Morimae, the leading expert in this field. The car models juxtaposed with the bonsai created a landscape in which the mock-ups served as *suiseki*, or "viewing stones." With this surprise approach, we aimed to pique visitors' interest in the philosophy of making things, and then transfer that interest to the white showpieces. Thus began the exhibition *JAPAN CAR: Designs for the Crowded Globe.*

Transportation: Desire and the Future

When thinking about the future of transportation, it is nonsense to assume that it will only come from technological progress or material innovation. It's not only technology that changes the environment. Technological advances are certainly a major factor, but people's desires – "What do I want this to be?" "How do I want to travel?" – are prime drivers of change as well.

For instance, the invention of the engine is a product of the innovative technological leap of converting the explosive

JAPAN CAR: Designs for the Crowded Globe at the Science Museum,
London: exhibition entrance and small-scale distorted models of cars

combustion of gasoline into propulsive power. But if there had not been a fundamental longing for the new power of speed, a machine fulfilling that desire would never have come into being. By controlling the force born from combustion as if taming a wild horse, by harnessing unprecedented speed in a single stroke, it became possible to cover distances never attained before by humans. Automobiles offered us the pleasure of moving freely and quickly. Even if the invention led to a new sort of death – by car crash. And even if the movements of these foreign objects trampled nature and impeded pedestrians, the human desire for transportation and greater mobility is so strong that we have resigned ourselves to these many negative factors.

The car is fruit grown in the soil of the desire for speed. Tokyo's Shuto Expressway, undulating like a great concrete snake, reflects the desires of the city's residents. Our forebears would not only have been surprised at the technology involved, but would probably also have been dismayed at the road's intrusiveness, shocked at the fact that the human desire for speed should surpass the desire to live in a beautiful city. In postwar Japan, we could not afford to conceive of the lifestyle that went with the new pleasures associated with the automobile, as illustrated by the *Michelin Guide* to hotels and restaurants. We were engrossed in rebuilding, and in maintaining a foothold among the advanced nations of the world. Perhaps there was also a national desire for a high-speed urban travel system. One took shape around the 1964 Tokyo Olympics; the Shuto Expressway rose above the city's houses and across its rivers.

Today, however, Japan's cars are beginning to change, because the attitude toward movement is changing. Lowering carbon dioxide emissions has become a global issue, and the fundamentals of automobile technology, from gasoline engines to electric motors and other alternatives, are themselves in transition. The entire urban system is changing, including transportation and communications, affecting everything in our environment.

One important side effect of this is the sharing of transportation information. We all know that a car's location can be accurately determined with GPS technology using satellites. But the need to protect the location of a car as private data has made it difficult to utilize that information. Yet seen from a macro point of view, the data has many positive uses, which could be shared to relieve traffic congestion, preventing blood from pooling in the veins of the "body" that is the city and smoothing its circulation. In addition to automobile manufacturers, participants in the *JAPAN CAR* exhibition included a company that provides large-scale technology for urban infrastructure as well as a firm that works on technologies aimed at the evolution of

Cars carrying GPS systems have begun to be used as sensors to track road congestion.

human–machine interaction. Hitachi, for instance, used GPS data recordings at thirty-second intervals, taken from a company's three thousand taxis on a given day, to create a video accurately visualizing the city's "blood flow." Each taxi became a point of light, and the image of the Tokyo metropolitan area radiating out from the Imperial Palace was precisely the image of a circulatory system with the heart at its center.

From the standpoint of developing human–car interaction, Denso presented the outline of a new conversation between driver and vehicle and demonstrated the capacity of sensors to detect information in the car's vicinity with precision far beyond that of the human eye.

Research on technology designed to prevent collisions is also making steady progress, and it is predicted that in the not-too-distant future, cars will virtually cease crashing into one another. When the Shin Tomei Expressway is finished, we can expect the introduction of technology that makes hands-free driving safer than hands-on driving.

What follows is my vision for the future of transportation, developed while working on *JAPAN CAR: Designs for the Crowded Globe.*

By replacing the standard engine with an alternative motor, and replacing gasoline with electricity, the automobile will be fundamentally transformed. The gasoline engine is an aggressive machine; the driver, controlling it with his physical skill, tames it, making the speed his own, so that he can exult in the activity of "going." The electric car is more closely associated with the rational pursuit of "traveling smoothly" than with the subjectivity of "going." It is a machine that inhibits the driving – or engine-controlling – aesthetic, one operated according to a dispassionate will to travel in the shortest and most energy-efficient manner. This system even allows for the situation in which the driver is almost nodding off as the car arrives at its destination. In short, it is expected that technology will shift transportation from the "driving" paradigm, grounded in an active desire to pilot the vehicle, to the "mobile" paradigm, guided by the desire to travel safely and efficiently.

Although some form of transport will remain an integral part of our everyday lives, like the air around us, it will no longer be an object to be coveted or displayed. Because the very essence of all industry is making things in volume yet unconsciously desirable, the car industry will have to shift its focus. The main means of conveyance is likely to change from vehicles owned by individuals to something closer to urban infrastructure.

Nevertheless, there will always be people who find this situation boring and prefer sports cars and powerful engines. So perhaps, despite its diminishing importance, the driver-oriented car will not entirely lose its luster as a symbol of the individuality of transportation. But because the rate of development will slow down, driving cars with conventional engines will come to be seen as a somewhat dangerous hobby. Someday, people may shudder at the fact that there was a time when all driving was left to faulty human beings, dependent on the guidance of white lines painted on the road. When that happens, we won't easily return to the reckless act of driving cars with combustion engines. Maybe inviting someone for a ride in that kind of car will even, if accepted, be regarded as a sign of trust – almost romantic!

On the other hand, leisure vehicles will evolve that reflect an increasing interest in a nature-oriented lifestyle. The urge to escape into the wild, with no traces of the artificial around – while still resorting to the benefits of advanced technology – is a not uncommon wish. It's one of the fundamental inclinations of human beings, so arrogant in their powers of reason. It shares something of the same motives that drove Westerners in the heyday of colonization to enjoy, in the most extreme natural settings, full-course meals on white tablecloths, delivered by white-uniformed servants. My prediction is that if electricity becomes the dominant energy source, recreational vehicles (RVs) and the like will become higher-performance vehicles. Because cars will improve not only as transport but also as devices with increased communication capacity, habitability, and entertainment, some people may begin to use their vehicles as a form of accommodation, living and working in a non-urban setting.

In the cities, greater control would lead to an alleviation of traffic congestion, and there would also be a marked reduction in exhaust fumes. A driver's license would be needed only for particular cars. Young people, drawn to solitude, might be interested in "one-person machines." Bicycles and solo vehicles might create a new fad. All transport technology will be influenced by the benefits of a more leisurely pace. The industry as a whole won't be divided along lines such as passenger/commercial. New divisions such as driving/mobile, city/nature, and public/personal will gain credence.

Someday I'd like to conceptualize the possibilities for moving objects that wouldn't be extensions of current cars but would reflect future needs. Imagination, planning, and making the invisible visible are the distinctive characteristics of design. Of course, it wouldn't be just me thinking. I'm inspired to gather wisdom from around the world and quietly hold a "meeting of minds" about this.

Chapter 2

Simplicity and Emptiness:
The Genealogy of an Aesthetic

Sori Yanagi's Kettle

Items for daily use designed by Sori Yanagi are quietly attracting interest. For instance, his tea kettle. It's an ordinary kettle. Yet its impressive bearing convinces one that as far as kettles go, this is it.

Using a kettle is simple. Fill it with water and place it on the stove. Whether it's a gas or electric range, it makes no difference. When the water boils and steam rises from the spout, pour the hot water into a teapot or thermos. Yanagi's kettle is a superbly designed tool for performing this sort of daily activity naturally and effortlessly. The grip of the handle and the sculpting of the ample spout have a bluntness – in a good sense – and a feeling of security. In the kettle's stout body, its solid stance, and the roundness of the lid, we sense the good faith of a designer devoting himself to the beauty of utility. Until recently, geometric, hard-edged Italian-made kettles somehow drew our attention, making us feel they were in the vanguard. But lately such designs look rather out of date.

The aesthetic appreciation of a kettle like Yanagi's is in no way nostalgia for the good old days or part of a retro boom. I believe that the obsession with novelty driven by our appetite for consumption has subsided and, as our temperature returns to normal, we have the freedom to survey our everyday surroundings honestly. Yanagi's kettle is popular because it is a completely ordinary industrial product that fits perfectly into our daily activities.

I once visited Yanagi at his atelier, and found many plaster models of products on display. These full-scale plaster models, which he crafted without the use of computer simulation, carefully and repeatedly reshaping them by gently rubbing them by hand, reflected his determined pursuit of form adapted to utility; I felt great respect for that conscientious approach and unwavering conviction. It is a welcome sign that these products have begun to be accepted again in the market.

Design is not styling. The act of systematically and deliberately creating the shape of an object is certainly design, but design is not merely that. Design is not only thought concerned with creation, but also a mode of thought in which the essence of a lifestyle or environment is conveyed through the medium of objects. Accordingly, the true purpose of design has as much to do with insight as it does with creating.

Everything around us has been designed. Drinking glasses, fluorescent lights, ballpoint pens, mobile phones, floor tiles, the arrangement of the holes in shower heads, the curls of instant noodles – in the sense of having been planned and produced, everything can be said to have been designed. Human beings form their environment by living. The real pleasure of design is in the process of awakening gradually to the multitude of accumulated insights interwoven with that environment. We see the world afresh when we grasp these threads, hitherto unnoticed.

Humans have designed their world in rectangles. We have divided the organic earth into rectangles, laying down rectangular streets lined with rectangular buildings. We enter these buildings through rectangular doors, and ascend and descend in rectangular elevators. Turning right angles down rectangular hallways, we open rectangular doors to reveal rectangular rooms. Arranged inside are rectangular furnishings and windows. The tables and cabinets and televisions and their remote controls are all rectangular. On a rectangular desk, you depress rectangular keys on a rectangular computer, and print out characters or letters on rectangular sheets of paper. The envelope into which you place the paper is also rectangular, as is the stamp affixed to the envelope. The postmark, however, may be round.

Why have we designed our world like this? You find very few rectangles in nature. The mathematics of four is not unknown in nature, but because the square is very unstable, there seem to be few concrete examples of it. In rare cases mineral crystals form perfect cubes, but these subtleties of creation appear rather artificial.

The origin of the great diversity of rectangular forms brought into being by humankind probably lies in the discovery and application of the straight line and the right angle. Both are comparatively easy to make with our hands. If you fold a big leaf, such as a banana leaf, in two, the crease becomes a straight line. Fold it again along the crease and you get a right angle. The extension of that is a rectangle. In other words, the rectangle is perhaps the most efficient form or geometric principle within our grasp, and explains why this classic form is still embodied in the latest personal computers and mobile phones. The monolith, the symbol of intellect featured in Stanley Kubrick's film *2001: A Space Odyssey* (1968), was a black rectangular panel.

The circle is another shape we like. The ritual mirrors of ancient Japan, coins, buttons, rice bowls, and CDs are all perfect circles. Although I was amazed when I saw a circle flawlessly hollowed out of the center of a piece of Mesopotamian stoneware, I realized that by rotating a hard stone like a drill into a softer stone, you can create a hole that is almost perfectly circular. Perhaps this, too, is because our two hands, adapted to the motion of rotation, sought out a perfect circle before intellectual inference or deductive reasoning did. In any case, simple geometric forms are the basis for acquiring rational insights into the relationship between humans and the world. Guided by the rectangle, we have designed a rectangular environment. Similarly inspired by the circle, we have applied it to numerous daily necessities.

Manhole covers are round, not rectangular. If they were rectangular, they might fall inside. In the same sense, paper must be rectangular. If it were round, there would be waste. The width-to-height ratio of standard paper sizes ensures that no matter how many times you fold a piece of paper, the proportions remain the same.

The cross section of most pencils is hexagonal, and of course there's a reason for this. If it were round, it could easily roll off a desk and snap its soft graphite tip. To avoid this, a shape that steadies it is needed. While a pencil with a triangular or square cross section would be firmer, it would be uncomfortable to hold. Accordingly, we have settled on a hexagonal shape that doesn't roll easily, is reasonably comfortable to hold, and is suitable for mass production, being bilaterally symmetrical.

A ball is round. Baseballs, tennis balls, and soccer balls are all round. One might think it's obvious why balls are this shape, but they weren't round from the outset. The technology for producing a highly accurate sphere is completely different from that of boring a round hole into stone. Early balls were not very precise spheres. But, apart from rugby and American football, games with an uneven ball aren't much fun. According to sports anthropologists, the development of modern science and the development of ball games advanced in parallel. The movement of a sphere is a clear representation of the laws of physics, and by playing ball games, in which they control the movements of spheres, humans reconfirm the natural order and laws of physics they have come to know. Along with advances in technical precision required to produce such an object, technical skill in the games themselves has also improved. Without spherical balls, such progress is impossible. If the ball's reaction to the same movement is not consistent, the pitcher can't learn to throw a forkball, and the acrobat can't mount a large ball and walk on it.

The relationship between ball and ball game is analogous to that between objects and lifestyle. Yanagi's kettle is an example: just as a high-precision ball represents the principles of the universe, outstanding design represents the principles of human behavior. The premise behind the statement that design is not mere styling is that, just as games won't improve if the equipment doesn't improve, neither lifestyle nor culture will mature if design doesn't cohere to the fundamentals of human behavior. Designers cognizant of this fact work to discover form as if creating a perfect ball. Le Corbusier, who stated that a house is a machine for living in; product designer Achille Castiglioni, who helped lead Italy to its position as a design powerhouse; Dieter Rams, who for a time represented the intellectual perfection of German industrial design; and Japan's Sori Yanagi all had the same objective: the quest for forms that illuminate life.

Sori Yanagi's father, Soetsu Yanagi, was the founder in 1926 of Japan's Mingei (folk craft) movement. In Mingei theory, the basis for the forms of common tools and utensils is to be found in the gradual accumulation of experience in daily life over long periods of time. Just as drips of water infused with calcite form stalactites in caves, the repetition of daily activities nurtures form. Behavior gives tools the inevitability of their shapes.

I feel deep sympathy with this point of view, but we can't resign ourselves to waiting hundreds of years for the flow of water to take effect. A technological revolution confronts us simultaneously with speed and change. What is needed is the will to employ our reason in crafting a future environment. This idea of building up an environment through the creation of forms made with intention came about simultaneously with the establishment of modern society. This is design. Design is not related to the concept of the accumulation of wealth. Its goal is to create a type of richness that can't be achieved merely through rapid economic growth. We would do well to continuously reflect on this idea.

Today, I wonder if we are succeeding in making the ball round. I brood about it, looking at Yanagi's squat, blunt kettle.

The Origin of "Simple"

The word "simple" is often used in Japan to indicate a neat or straightforward appearance or a condition of concision and consistency. Generally, it is used in a favorable sense. Expressions like "a simple life" or "simple is best" are commonplace. You might have to be a bit "simple-minded" not to mind being called that – but perhaps a simple mind is better than a confused and complicated one.

But when did the word, or the concept of "simple," take on its current meaning? When did simplicity as a value or an aesthetic take hold in society as a favorable notion? I would argue that its origin dates back to about 150 years ago. Let me explain why I think this.

Were objects simple when making them wasn't yet complicated – before human beings created complex designs and patterns? Most Stone Age tools have straightforward shapes. But the people of the Stone Age certainly can't have seen them as simple. The concept of simplicity is premised on its opposite. Early stone tools certainly have relatively simple shapes, but those who made them were not aiming for purity or minimalism. A lack of complexity under circumstances in which complex shapes could not be produced should instead be described as primitive or rudimentary. To repeat, simplicity is a concept to be understood in opposition to complexity, redundancy, and excess. Thus, the emergence of simplicity comes at a much later time in our long history.

Culture emerges with complexity. Take bronze artifacts,

for instance. Those unearthed from the ruins of Yin, capital of the ancient Chinese Shang dynasty (1600–1046 BCE), are very complex in form. One might assume these pieces to be the product of a gradual evolution from simple to complicated, but except for some examples that predate the Shang dynasty, simply shaped bronze pieces are seldom found. Almost from their onset, Chinese bronzes had complicated shapes with elaborate surface decoration. The bronze vessels have exaggerated spouts and handles, and their surfaces are also densely covered with fine spiral patterns. Why?

Bronze is an alloy of copper and tin. Adding tin reduces the melting point and also makes the resulting alloy harder. Compared to other ancient civilizations, China was relatively late to work with bronze; it was the high-tech material of that era. Even today, bronze casting is not simple. Bronze vessels could not have been produced without the investment of an astonishing amount of time and attention by highly skilled artisans and technicians, and the intricate patterns adorning these pieces indicate that complexity was deliberately explored as a goal.

Furthermore, we can speculate what lay behind such diligence and precision. The larger bronze vessels can't even be lifted. Clearly they weren't intended for practical use, but meant as objects designed to inspire reverence and awe. They should not be dismissed simply as "ritual vessels," however.

Generally, when people form a group, be it a village or a state, a strong centripetal force is needed to maintain unity. The hegemony at the center must have firm command; if weak, it will be supplanted by something or someone with greater power, or the group will be absorbed by a stronger group. Societies are like spinning tops. Without sufficient centripetal force, they collapse. We may imagine that the complex bronze vessels manifested this force in visually appealing forms. These dazzling bronze objects no doubt made ordinary people gasp in admiration, and must have assumed this tacit role.

Following the collapse of the Shang and Zhou dynasties, China entered the Spring and Autumn and the Warring States periods, during which there was rivalry between warlords in different regions. The slightest inattention could lead to invasion by a neighboring state. Accordingly, the ruler and his ministers had to be shrewd, and their troops disciplined. It is believed that out of this tension arose the wisdom of the Hundred Schools of Thought: philosophies that flourished from the sixth century BCE to 221 BCE. The surfaces of cast bronzes were crowded with Chinese characters; decorative motifs found their way even onto arms and armor, inspiring dread and commanding respect in those exposed to their magnificence and mystery. Motifs such as dragons were ideal responses to this demand. It should be noted, however, that the dragons evolved from the tightly engraved spiral patterns on the surface of Shang dynasty bronzes, which began to be seen as imaginary animals. The dragon motif was neither something deliberately drawn to represent a monster from a folk tale, nor something derived from religious beliefs. It was a decorative pattern meant to bestow majesty to the surface of an object that took on the likeness of an animal. And since the concentration

Left and above right: Bronze vessel, Shang dynasty, China (Museum of East Asian Art, Cologne) Below right: Ceiling of the Hall of Prayer for Good Harvests, Temple of Heaven, 1406–20, Beijing

of markings completely covered the object, dragons soon entwined themselves around and enveloped the surfaces of many organic forms and columns.

Something similar may be observed in the Islamic cultural sphere. Idolatry is strictly prohibited in Islam, so instead of representational images like dragons, geometric patterns and arabesque designs were developed to an unusual degree, and cover the surfaces of royal palaces and mosques.

Aggressive-looking tattoos are meant to intimidate the viewer. The banning of tattooed individuals from public baths and other facilities in Japan probably stems from a desire to protect the public from the aura of menace that tattoos can project. Dragon motifs in China and geometric patterns in Islam also seem intended to project power, expressed in the intensity of the dense patterning.

It is the same in India. The white marble Taj Mahal is an architectural marvel built by the Mughal emperor Shah Jahan in memory of his cherished wife. The surface is densely covered with patterned inlays of colorful stones collected from all over the world. The inlay technique is achieved through a sequence of amazingly complex processes by which the surface of the substrate stone is incised with decorative patterns that are matched and filled with precisely carved and differently colored tesserae. Even today this ornamentation inspires a sense of wonder and conveys the power of Shah Jahan.

In Europe, the opulent, expansive Baroque and Rococo decorative styles reached their zenith during the reign of Louis XIV, France's Sun King, the greatest of the absolute monarchs. The Hall of Mirrors in the Palace of Versailles is said to be where royal audiences took place. Imagining myself walking down that red carpet to face the king leaves me paralyzed with fear. This is not because I'm a cowardly person. It's because the Hall of Mirrors was designed to intimidate people.

In eras when sheer power ruled the world and competition among powers created instability in society, the artifacts of a culture were exhibited as symbols of power. Power created a hierarchy in society, which in turn created a hierarchy of ornamentation,

Left: Sheikh Lotfollah Mosque, 1603–19, Iran
Above right: Taj Mahal, 1632–53, India
Below right: Hall of Mirrors, 1678–84, Palace of Versailles, France

in the context of which simplicity signified nothing but a deficit of power.

Change finally came under the aegis of modernity. With the modernization of society, standards of value were reorganized around the idea of greater freedom, with the state becoming part of the essential framework of services supporting its citizens. History has seen a succession of many different experiments in the way nations and regimes should function, but generally speaking, the world has steered a clear course toward a society founded upon the equal rights of all people to live fulfilling lives.

Conforming to this course, it was no longer necessary for objects to serve as symbols of power. A chair no longer needed to express the status of its owner; it only needed to provide a place to sit. The development of science also helped promote a more rational approach to design. Before long, the curves of the cabriole-legged chair became unnecessary and the embellishments of Baroque and Rococo styles became relics of the past. The association between resources and humans and the relationship between objects and functions were recalculated in a more straightforward way, and through the efficient application of resources and labor, a new formal beauty was discovered: simplicity.

The world of a century and a half ago does not stand out as a historical period. In the mid-nineteenth century Europe was energized by the Industrial Revolution, the fruits of which were assembled for the Great Exposition at the cast-iron and glass Crystal Palace in London. At about this time in Austria, Thonet began to use bentwood techniques to mass-produce simple, functional chairs for the popular market. Meanwhile, in Great Britain, Darwin created a sensation with *The Origin of Species*. In Japan, which had shut itself off from the outside world for more than two centuries, the arrival of the "black ships" of the West touched off a movement advocating reverence for the emperor and the expulsion of foreigners. There is no particular moment when the age of simplicity began, but I think it was roughly around this time that the value of simplicity began to kindle a new light of reason in people's minds.

Marking the end of the long era in which power was

Left: Louis XV style armchair
Right: Cesca armchair, 1928, designed by
Marcel Breuer, manufactured by Thonet

expressed as complexity, an honest pursuit of new lifestyles led to a reconception of furniture, houses, cities, and roads. Modernism was the process in which objects sloughed off their extravagant skins. Wealth and cupidity often obscure the essence of things. People sometimes tire of modesty, and tend toward decadence. But taking a close look at the nature of things today, it is fair to say that the world still revolves on the axis of simplicity.

The Richness of Nothingness

It was at the Raku Museum in Kyoto that I first saw Chojiro's Raku bowl, made for use in the tea ceremony. The impact is still etched clearly in my mind. Enthralled by that black, rounded bowl, I stared at it for so long that my breath clouded the glass of the display case. It was like a lump of darkness that had absorbed all meaning and energy into its mute self. While the universe is apparently expanding infinitely, perhaps this is what it would look like if it contracted into itself. Its shape is concise and pure, but could never be described as simple. In it lives a different kind of aesthetic, inaccessible to reason.

The simplicity central to the Japanese cultural aesthetic did not arrive along the same path as the concept of "the simple" in Western aesthetics, which appeared toward the end of the nineteenth century. Looking back on the history of Japan, several hundred years before that time, one finds forms – exemplified by Chojiro's tea bowl and the Dojinsai, the shogun Ashikaga Yoshimasa's study in Kyoto's Jishoji temple – that express a strength of purity and concision pitted against complexity; yet they differ essentially from the Western concept of "simple." How? In their emptiness, I would assert. This quality is not accidental. It is created with consciousness and intention. Through its very emptiness, a vessel can apply a centripetal force absorbing one's awareness.

When I first encountered Raku tea bowls, I was working on an advertising photo shoot in tea rooms in Kyoto. Our locations included the Dojinsai study and Togudo hall at Jishoji temple, the Sa-an tea house in the Gyokurin-in subtemple of Daitokuji, and the Kankyu-an tea house of Mushanokoji Senke, one of the tea ceremony schools – all of which are assets designated as national treasures or important cultural properties. Experiencing them first-hand, I found a vibrant connection between the aesthetic they represented and my own sensibility as a designer today. It was the Dojinsai study at Jishoji (popularly known as the Silver Pavilion), in the Higashiyama district of Kyoto, where Ashikaga Yoshimasa spent his last years, that particularly affected me.

Yoshimasa began his secluded retirement there at the end of the Muromachi period, more than five hundred years ago. A little later, in the second half of the sixteenth century, the tea master Sen no Rikyu was engaged in refining Higashiyama culture through the tea ceremony (*chanoyu*). All this was more than three hundred years before the Bauhaus was founded. Aesthetic lineages grounded in simplicity are rare, because the world has been dazzled by complexity, by the conflict among various representations of power.

There must have been a good underlying reason for this radical shift of consciousness away from complexity toward the concise and elemental. I believe that the Onin War (1467–77), which resulted in the destruction by fire of many of Kyoto's cultural assets, was the turning point.

Ashikaga Yoshimasa, the eighth Muromachi shogun, was little interested in ruling. A lover of architecture and the arts, he reportedly indulged in these interests to the point that the power of the shogunate declined. If he had been a more energetic ruler, dealt more skillfully with the problem of succession, and united his family, his reign might not have lapsed into chaos and the Onin War might never have occurred. Yet paradoxically, while his feeble grasp of politics led to confusion, unrest, and war, these factors created the conditions that allowed Japanese culture to mature and make progress toward originality.

The Onin War was an almost unimaginably protracted struggle that exposed the fundamental weakness of the prevailing shogunate. The fires of the nearly decade-long war that assailed Kyoto, with its concentration of historical sites, caused catastrophic cultural damage.

Because Kyoto escaped bombing during World War II, elderly Kyoto citizens sometimes mean the Onin War when they speak of "the last war." This gives it an almost elegant ring, but the nature of destruction hasn't changed. Just as Tokyo was almost completely leveled by incendiary bombs dropped from B-29s in 1945, most of Kyoto was destroyed by fire at the end of the Muromachi period. Unlike the fire-bombings of World War II, however, the aggression in Kyoto was accompanied by vandalism and looting. Even the imperial palace and the residences of the shogunal officials and the nobility were razed or plundered. A tremendous number of irreplaceable treasures were lost at this time, from Buddhist temples and images to villas, gardens, picture scrolls, books, and textiles. The damage was so great that Japan's centuries-old culture would have to be reshaped.

It seems that Yoshimasa's pursuit of beauty was so unbalanced that even when the fighting approached within a hundred meters of where he was, he was engrossed in his calligraphy and paintings. Conversely, he must have understood all the more keenly the enormity of the loss of cultural properties in the war, which today's connoisseurs would still covet. Eventually, he retired from the office of shogun, ceding the title to his son, but he never ceased his involvement in art and architecture, culminating in his ingeniously designed retirement villa, Higashiyama Goten, on the present site of Jishoji temple. From this would bloom a thoroughly new Japanese sensibility.

One would assume that finances were tight when Yoshimasa's villa was built, immediately after the fighting, but he was not the type to practice frugality even in such circumstances. Putting aside the responsibilities of ruling his people, investing as much money as he could, he created a place in which to find repose during his final years.

Yoshimasa did not express himself in extravagance, however; it was beauty honoring concision and purity he sought after. Four and a half tatami mats, carefully laid out; shoji screens filtering sunlight into soft indirect light; *fusuma* sliding panels retaining the grace and tautness of the paper stretched across them; a writing desk and a display shelf tucked neatly into one corner of the room. Open the shoji in front of the desk and the scenery of the garden appears before one's eyes, sliced into the proportions of a hanging scroll. These things are as beautiful as mathematical propositions. Yoshimasa did not choose this form of expression as a humble retreat from the world. It's likely that having pursued the arts at the height of his political power and then experienced the great losses of the Onin War, he had grasped the basis of a new sensibility.

Until that time, Japan's art and furnishings had never been plain and simple. Situated at the eastern edge of the Eurasian continent, Japan had welcomed the influences of other cultures.

Fascinated by and able to import the splendid symbolic objects created by great powers beyond its borders, Japan assumed more of the ostentatious aspects of those cultures than one might think. Emblematic of this was the flourishing of an imported Buddhist culture and the magnificent cultural events associated with it, such as the ceremonies held to consecrate newly constructed Buddha images. Japanese culture developed out of admiration for the intricacy and novelty of ornamentation embodied in these imported objects, and the immense amount that could be learned and absorbed from them.

Today there is no way of knowing what kinds of images whirled through the minds of eyewitnesses to the destruction of the cultural metropolis of Kyoto, or what sort of philosophical views arose in response. But I think that there must have been a surge of resistance to the idea of retracing and restoring the details of splendid ornamentation that went before and a strong inclination toward its opposite – a completely new aesthetic embracing plainness and neutrality. This surely is how an aesthetic of emptiness began. It was a revolution in Japanese sensibilities – spare, cool, and dry.

The custom of drinking tea is found throughout the world. I believe that both the act of drinking warm, fragrant tea and the way we spend time doing it attest to a delight in life. The tea ceremony (*chanoyu*), which originated in the latter half of the Muromachi period, is a particularly subtle example of this universal custom. To me, the scope it offers is what makes it special. It is simply an excuse, or an opportunity: the bare tea room is an emptiness in which people's feelings and imagination can evolve through the minimal preparations for enjoying tea. These might include floating some cherry petals in a bowl of water, giving the host and guests the illusion of sitting beneath cherry trees in full bloom; or feeling a cool summer breeze in the taste of a jelly sweet. In these associations lies the real pleasure of *chanoyu*. The focus is not the reproduction of images, but rather the creativity of *mitate*, or metaphor, which, through constraint and absence, encourages the guest to make associations, drawing on images from their own imagination.

From this perspective of emptiness, the allegory of the emperor's new clothes can be interpreted in the opposite sense. The creativity of *chanoyu* lies in imaginatively clothing the emperor who appeared naked to the eye of a child, letting him wear "nothing" in full confidence. Because there is nothing, he can accept any and all *mitate*.

This is also true in ikebana (flower arrangement), which quietly creates a negative space in which a certain tension is evoked, and Japanese garden design, which stimulates human emotion at the interface between the natural and the artificial. The tautness of sensation that these practices have in common originates in the dynamics of "emptiness," which invites our imagination to expand. Working on a photo shoot in rooms designed for the tea ceremony, I experienced that effect, confirming for myself an aesthetic vein flowing through our sensibilities in such places. I understood Western modernism and simplicity but felt there was something different going on in Japan – and

that suspicion was confirmed through this experience.

    Encountering Chojiro's tea bowls at the Raku Museum marked the completion of my discovery of the dynamics of emptiness. Dropping by the museum after finishing the day's work, I saw an array of objects into which everything in the universe seemed to be distilled.

Dojinsai, Ashikaga Yoshimasa's study, Jishoji (Silver Pavilion), Kyoto
Photo: Yoshihiko Ueda

Ami-shu and Design

When did designers whose work is not only to create an aesthetic but also to apply it begin to play a professional role in Japan? I can't help thinking of the group of people called *ami-shu* (or *doboshu*), who became prominent around the Muromachi period and whose vocation was akin to that of today's designers.

Ami was originally used for the Buddhist names of the monks who belonged to Jishu, one of the schools of the Pure Land sect. Jishu monks also accompanied armies into battle, where they offered *nembutsu*, or Buddhist prayers, for the spirits of fallen warriors and took care of a series of arrangements for them to achieve rebirth in the Pure Land. But it seems likely that they were not limited to this role; they probably also dealt with medical care of the wounded, miscellaneous chores, and, being proficient in the arts, activities with an artistic aspect.

In time, even those who were not members of the Jishu clergy began to attach the suffix *ami* to their names. Individuals who were appointed to responsible positions in influential samurai houses to look after things artistic, among other duties, came to be referred to by this or a similar term, *doboshu*.

Culture always lives in connection or contention with the power of the day, whether military, economic, political, or populist, serving to add luster or distract. Power desires aesthetics as a sensory polish to erase the impurities and poisons ensuing from that power. Whether or not that desire should be called the origin of culture, there have always been people prepared to make an aesthetic response to that demand. To keep in touch with the arts is to be permanently conscious of the fact that there is another focus that inspires human sensibility, operating on a different level from the prevailing authority. Invariably, a subtle conflict arises between living a life in which sensibility and aesthetics are in mutual rapport and serving the power of the day by providing aesthetic polish.

Catering to this "client" is an obvious stimulus to skill and talent, but the refinement cultivated in people involved in aesthetic management inevitably matures to the point of surpassing the client's expectations. Be it under the Ashikaga shogunate or the corporations that have reigned supreme under capitalism, I feel an innate sympathy with those who share my situation of responding, half in accommodation and half in resistance, to the desire of the powerful for a more refined image.

The Japanese fine arts – poetry, calligraphy, and painting – originated in the pastimes of emperors and aristocrats; high-ranking individuals played leading roles in composing poetry and writing it down. The realm of aesthetics existed as an accomplishment that only the elite, equipped from childhood with rarified information and knowledge, could pursue. However, as time went on, a separation developed between the aspiration to pursue the arts and the technical skills needed to practice them. Recognition gradually spread that the ability to create beautiful things was not due to status or birth, but rather to innate talent and special training. This was the course of events that led to the advancement, from the Heian (794–1192) to the Kamakura period (1192–1333), of highly trained individuals such as *miya daiku* (carpenters specializing in temple and shrine construction), engravers, and painters. The *ami-shu* of the Muromachi period, however, had talents that were somewhat different in spirit from those of artists and craftsmen. Talent not only for producing paintings and sculptures, but also for exhibiting an aesthetic through direction and arrangement, began to play an active role.

Art forms established during the Muromachi period include Noh drama, *renga* collaborative poetry, the earliest type of ikebana (*tatehana*), *chanoyu*, landscape gardening, and the construction of *shoin* (studies) and tea rooms. All these artistic achievements were enlivened by a talent held by a group of professionals not only for creating artistic objects, but also for arranging them into an experience.

There is a word, *tonseisha*, indicating someone who withdraws from the world to follow the path of Buddhism. In any era, people who create art and live off the proceeds lead an existence that deviates from normal social practices and from respectable occupations. Making a living from a talent of this sort often means presenting oneself to society as a proper noun – a "name" – and depends on abilities that vary with the individual and can't be easily transmitted or inherited. In the *ami-shu*'s talent, which led to some becoming "names" among the clients of Muromachi society, I see here the origin of Japan's designers, in the sense that they were agents of a variety of cultural activities that differ from pure art.

When we speak of the *ami-shu*, names like Kanami (1333–1384) and Zeami (1363–1443) in the Noh theater, Ryuami in *tatehana* flower arrangement, Zenami in gardening, and the art connoisseur Noami immediately come to mind. Interestingly, Zenami came from a very humble background; but his exceptional gift for making artificial mountains, channeling water, installing stones, and arranging trees and shrubs made him a favorite of Ashikaga Yoshimasa, who had a passion for gardening. When Zenami was ill, Yoshimasa personally administered his medicine and even offered prayers for his recovery.

How the *ami-shu* behaved in response to the shogun's patronage is perhaps revealing. It was Yoshimasa's idea to send his gardeners to Ichijoin, a branch temple of Nara's Kofukuji, to procure some trees. The priests, however, resented the way the gardeners helped themselves to trees in the temple garden as if they owned the place, and aggressively drove them away. In retaliation, Yoshimasa ordered the temple's territory to be confiscated. The temple then apologized and offered a settlement. This incident gives a little glimpse into how privileged the *ami-shu* must have felt.

There is another anecdote. In those days the custom was gradually becoming established of displaying flowers as a *zashiki-kazari*, the arrangement of decorative objects in the *tokonoma*, the alcove in a traditional Japanese room. Flowers had been displayed in vases from ancient times, but this was an age when the technique of arranging them according to a set aesthetic matured. Among those who practiced this art, it was Ryuami who earned renown. Apparently, Yoshimasa had complete faith in him. One day, a priest from Sokokuji brought Yoshimasa some plum blossoms and daffodils. Pleased, Yoshimasa ordered Ryuami to arrange them. Ryuami was ill and refused. Yoshimasa, not backing down, gave him a strict command, and Ryuami complied, producing a wonderful arrangement. The shogun's obstinacy is one thing, but

Ryuami's own behavior shows a surprising independence of mind for someone in his position.

Whether for the creation of gardens or the arrangement of flowers, Yoshimasa could not be expected to indicate anything with sketches or plans. It was the *ami-shu* who placed stones, made artificial hills, planted trees, grew plants, arranged flowers, served tea, judged the quality of imported articles, and designed sophisticated interiors. And it was the interaction between a cultural director like Yoshimasa and these privileged designers that contributed to the unique aesthetic – the spare, cool, dry qualities mentioned in the preceding section – that came into being. The sensibilities of influential cultural leaders like Yoshimasa were steadily enriched through these interactions. Something of this relationship may linger in the way that today's designers shun the conventional clothes – the necktie, or suit – worn by other working men and women.

Chapter 3

Houses: Refining the Home

The Shape of Living

As discussed in the previous chapter, simplicity is central to Japanese aesthetics. The sensibility that values simplicity and emptiness developed after the Onin War, when the preference for the ostentation of imported products was wiped away by the loss of cultural assets. New values emerged and were refined not only by those of noble status and temporal power, but also by many talented individuals dealing in the realm of beauty. The sensibility they developed was continuously transmitted at the deepest levels of Japan's culture, through the long and stable Edo period (1603–1867), the period of Westernization following the Meiji Restoration (1868), and then through the postwar influx of American culture. This sensibility constitutes the core of Japanese aesthetics, based on the principles of delicacy, thoroughness, precision, and simplicity.

The Japanese archipelago is characterized by its isolation, situated on the eastern edge of Asia and separated from the mainland by the Sea of Japan. Its citizens share a unique language; they also tend to have trouble mastering foreign languages like English. These factors have actually functioned as cultural breakwaters protecting Japan's originality. From the mid-nineteenth to the twentieth century, the concept of a modern society based on individual freedom and Western civilization and founded on the Industrial Revolution swept the globe. Japan had to not only accept these influences, but, despite the resulting chaos, also open itself to the wisdom of the world and adapt. There is a sophistication that cannot be attained without riding the waves of such chaos. After the rapid postwar economic growth, Japanese today seem to have lost their sense of hunger; their fighting spirit and ambition have slumped. However, I believe that this is precisely the moment at which we will be able to move toward refinement, with a slight sense of tranquility.

The other day I dropped by the Museum of Oriental Ceramics in Osaka, where I had the chance to survey their vast collection of Asian ceramics. Looking at the museum displays, I was able to better understand the fascination with ceramics as a material achievement through history, as well as the distribution of manufacturing power in East Asia. In a striking map of historic kiln sites, density decreases in this order: China, Korea, Japan. The map shows that a tremendous number of ceramics were produced across the whole eastern part of China; it also shows how ceramics culture matured in the unique topography of the Korean peninsula.

Japan, an island nation at the edge of Asia, proved that it could build on the advantages of Western civilization, which had pioneered the modern age. In recent decades, countries across Asia have achieved high standards of production – not only of ceramics. The changes in China have been remarkable. Fueling its explosive growth are the fact that China itself constitutes a gigantic economic bloc, and moreover, the Chinese people understand their country's potential for massive growth and have a burning motivation to advance. The cheap labor force is only one of the factors contributing to the country's success;

China also has the advantages of a strong work ethic, advanced technological strength and product quality, ambitious research, improvements in efficiency, overwhelming scale, and abundant investment from all over the world. In Japan there are nineteen cities with populations over 500,000. In China there are 185 such cities, and in fifteen years, there are expected to be nearly three hundred.

In South Korea, partly because its domestic market is small, there is a powerful desire to cultivate markets outside of the country, and they have focused their ambition to compete against foreign companies in terms of growth, much more than Japan used to. Unfortunately, after its period of high economic growth, Japan has grown soft and is having trouble attracting global attention with simple manufacturing.

But the value of a nation's culture doesn't depend on the number of products it makes. Japan should have recognized this during the heyday of "Made in Japan." After the real estate bubble burst, reflecting failed Japanese investments in U.S. real estate like Manhattan's historic Rockefeller Center, we should have realized that wealth alone cannot make us happy. Fulfillment and happiness are possible only when people have the wisdom to engage with the culture, investing in what they have. Of course, both the poverty of scarcity and the poverty of excess are problems, but having sung the praises of industrial production and the money game, we are now called upon to draw on our personal experiences, both bitter and sweet, to gain a broader perspective on the future of global economic culture. Not the near future –

we need to look at the future of about fifty years hence, while simultaneously reviewing our history from the present back to ancient times.

Japan is expected to lead the world in certain fields. Certainly, Japan's automobile industry will continue to be a world leader; mechanisms of transportation will transcend the individual vehicle, requiring automotive control technology that functions as an urban system. I think Japan may also demonstrate leadership in the electricity supply system represented by the smart grid; in the evolution of the home from a collection of individual appliances into a single large-scale, integrated appliance; and in environmental technology, as exemplified by solar power and the passive house.

I would like to present a vision of Japan's capacity for deploying its *quality* as a country of beauty through an application of the aesthetic that Japanese have preserved at a deep level, rather than operating from the perspective of *quantity* demanded by industry. This is because I believe that in the end, the level of aesthetics that can be applied to a technology determines the level that technology will reach.

I'd like to begin with a vision for the "shape of living" – the home. We Japanese ought to exhibit a more refined aesthetic for the home, an aesthetic centered on the simplicity that matured from the Muromachi period through the Momoyama period. Through the work of the *ami-shu*, the original designers and art directors, *shoin* architecture, gardens, flower arrangement, and the tea ceremony became more refined. The sensibility brewed in those times is infused into the deepest sensibilities of our daily lives. Precisely because the ikebana and *chanoyu* culture permeates the lives of common people, I enjoy a cordial and respectful welcome when I stay at a Japanese-style inn. How many nations can boast better service at their Western-style five-star hotels than we experience at these *ryokan*, where the proprietors serve their guests with the etiquette, banquet entertainment, and arrangement of space and furnishings unique to their nation?

But what about homes in general? I'd love to report that after passing through the lattice gate and following the stone path to the *genkan* entrance of a typical Japanese house, I remove my shoes before treading on the *agari kamachi* (a shallow step indicating the entrance to the home), and see, in a neatly swept, simple tatami-mat room, a scroll hung in the alcove and an arrangement of seasonal flowers. Unfortunately, that's not the case. I wouldn't say such places have disappeared entirely, but the reality of Japan's homes today is that most people live in condominiums, apartments, or public housing developments, surrounded by an enormous number of material things.

Japan steered a drastic course toward Westernization at the time of the Meiji Restoration (1868), but initially, modernization and Westernization didn't leave much of a mark on commoners' homes – which we will take as the standard for this discussion of "the shape of living." While the archetypical elements of the Japanese-style room – *fusuma* sliding panels, shoji screens, and tatami mats – were being established at the end of the Muromachi period, the masses were not living in *shoin* drawing rooms. Instead, a typical house had pillars sunk in the earth supporting a thatched roof, with straw mats spread on an earthen floor. Other residential styles developed, including private homes with magnificently engineered wood framing built on pillars placed on foundation stones, or the more informal version of the aristocratic *shoin-zukuri* style known as *sukiya,* which incorporated the tea ceremony aesthetic of *wabi,* or austere elegance. Although such homes were built for an affluent minority, they served as a medium for transmitting an uncompromising housing aesthetic to the popular level.

Gradually, commoners began to use tatami-mat rooms, and in the Edo period, there were more ordinary houses built with a four-room layout partitioned by *fusuma.* In such a home, there were few pieces of furniture, and furnishings and bedding were tucked away in closets or storage rooms so that the main rooms could be used as convertible spaces, both dining room and bedroom, for example. There was no progress toward functional specialization in Japanese living spaces. Most Japanese houses, whether extravagant or modest, were made of wood, and with the evolution of tools, the carpenter's techniques improved.

Both the Great Kanto Earthquake of 1923 and World War II resulted in large-scale loss of housing in Tokyo. Modern housing gradually began to take shape after the earthquake, thanks to the Dojunkai, a public housing corporation that erected concrete apartment complexes, and the research of architect Uzo Nishiyama, which defined the concept of the "nDK" apartment layout (n = # of bedrooms; DK = open-plan "dining kitchen").

Ordinary city dwellers thus began to experience the separation of eating and sleeping spaces. With rapid postwar economic growth and more salaried workers, the separation of work and life accelerated and public housing and condominiums began to be recognized as archetypes of urban housing. Accordingly, Japan's housing began to take on an air of bleak isolation from tradition and aesthetics. A deluge of uniformity begat a sort of resignation among the people.

What kind of future is there for housing in Japan? I see a lot of potential.

The Wisdom of Homemaking

No one teaches us how to make a home. I have no memory of being instructed by my father or my grandfather, "If you're in your mid-thirties, buy this kind of house, and furnish and equip it in such and such a way." This is not because my father was remiss or my grandfather cold. Over the past fifty years, there has been an upheaval in the Japanese lifestyle, so our generation lacks the wisdom of the generations that came before ours. The forms of the home, the family, and the community have all changed dramatically, and continue to change, moment to moment. That's why they don't teach us how to make a home, even in school. At most, we learn how to sew a dust cloth and the rudiments of cooking; in this precarious situation, students have no exposure to the guiding principles of homemaking.

All of a sudden you realize that realtors' flyers have

defined what people desire in a home. They're inserted in newspapers and seem to be everywhere. They've taught us the meaning of the 2LDK layout (a two-bedroom apartment with a open-plan living room, dining area, and kitchen) while simultaneously shocking us with extraordinary prices. As if buffeted by waves of inflation, floor plans that are far from spacious have been tagged with prices in the tens of millions of yen. I remember the gloom I felt when I encountered this fact while still a university student. As a young single person, I lived a modest lifestyle. Living in a six-mat apartment, working part-time to pay the rent, I was dazzled by the ads for "L" and "DK," but shocked by the prices.

I figured that if I got a job, with a salary that was a huge improvement over my part-time wages, I might net ¥400,000 a month. By economizing, I might put away ¥100,000 a month, and in a year, ¥1,200,000. But a condominium cost ¥40 million; I wouldn't have enough even if I saved for thirty years. I felt dejected.

I finished graduate school in 1983. The price of land had begun to rise steeply and steadily. Even now, I remember the copywriter Shigesato Itoi saying, "The interesting thing about Japan today is that even twenty million yen won't buy you a house." His wry remark was right on point.

We were compelled to prioritize our values. What kind of travel would twenty million yen fund? You could take a million-yen luxury trip annually for twenty years. The yen was strong; it would go further overseas. I might be able to live a much more dynamic life than if I bought a Japanese condo and lived a modest life without ever going anywhere. OK, I thought, I'll choose travel, even if it means I have to pay rent for the rest of my life. At the time, I didn't know if it was the right choice. Either way, with the balance between value and price beginning to spin out of control, I didn't feel like spending my money on what had become the established routine. It made no sense that it would take the better part of my entire life savings just to purchase an average home.

However, after the bubble burst and the economic environment leveled out, the land and housing situation changed too. When prices were doubling over twenty years, developers were preoccupied with how efficiently they could pack 2LDKs onto limited building sites. But that business model is coming to an end. Finally, living spaces are being evaluated for quality, rather than valued simply as real estate. Tokyo land prices have begun to come down and calm down, and gradually, they are reaching a level that makes building a house feasible once again.

Especially since the idea of gut renovation began to spread around the world, homebuilding in cities like Tokyo has reached a critical point. We've accumulated the wisdom, strategies, and institutions to make this possible, and in Japan, where there is an abundant supply of architecture that can last a century or more, a levelheaded movement to recycle and reuse is finally arising. If we think in terms of the skeleton, which can be used for a long time, and the infill, which is easier to alter, we realize it's best to acquire a high-quality skeleton, and then thoroughly renovate the infill to suit one's own lifestyle. With enough time and effort, it's possible to create a home that far surpasses a custom-built new house.

Fifty years ago, the average family had four members. Now it's 2.5. The single-person household is now the most common. In second place is the two-person household. Combined, these account for 60 percent of the total. The number of extended families that include grandparents is dropping sharply, and households of empty-nester couples and divorced single people are on the rise. These trends are certainly problematic, but pessimism alone won't lead to progress. This demographic development presents a new possibility for the Tokyo lifestyle. One plan does not fit all. Each person can come up with a "shape of living" to suit his or her own identity. Even if the outside of the apartment complex stays the same, a dazzling variety of interiors would count as luxury.

Since the Meiji Restoration, the Japanese people have been buffeted by Western civilization. They've experienced the depths of confusion and loss resulting from the Great Kanto Earthquake and defeat in war, but they have also achieved economic growth and maturity that is rare in the world. Japan today is not a country of homogeneous "salarymen." Individuals have begun to take a look at society and themselves, and to become aware of the idiosyncrasies in the way they work, the pace of their lives, their interests and hobbies. Sometimes they travel abroad, encountering the lifestyles of different cultural spheres, and they have begun to enrich themselves by recognizing an abundance that does not depend upon money. I wrote earlier that the quality of the soil influences the life force of the trees that grow there as well the form of the fruit they bear; it's only natural that today's Japanese desire a unique quality of life, one differing from that in Europe, the United States, or China. The soil of their desires is one permeated with the traditional aesthetics of delicacy, thoroughness, precision, and simplicity. Now it's time to cultivate and harvest a high-quality lifestyle.

How does one acquire a lifestyle with the perfect fit? How does one find a house in which one wants to live, inspired and motivated by one's own volition rather than a realtor's flyer? It's not that hard. Just close your eyes and go with your gut. You simply need to put what is most important to your life in the center of your house.

If you love a Japanese bath, don't put it in some unassuming location like they do in 2DK apartments, condominiums, or ordinary houses – get a splendid bathtub and put it in the sunniest place there is. You can actually make the entire home a bathing space. Then the bath is not a dank, dark space, but a bright, refreshing, open, spa-like living space. We can now make toilets and bathing areas as comfortable and clean as living rooms, all the more sensible for our traditional way of living, in which we remove our shoes before entering the home. In fact, the products of the leading toilet and bathtub manufacturers have begun evolving in that direction.

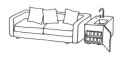

Someone who likes to play the piano should put a grand piano right in the middle of the room, lay soundproof flooring and erect soundproof walls, making a space to play the piano to your heart's content. It might also be convenient to have a spacious floor, like in a gym, where one can exercise. The owner of this house will be able to practice at his or her own pace, with no time constraints.

If you like to cook, invest in the kitchen, and make a home in which food is the centerpiece. Because you cook at home, you may be able to enjoy a luxurious lifestyle at relatively low cost. You'd be surprised at how well made some kitchens are. German and Italian system kitchens are expensive, but you can buy a kitchen instead of a Mercedes Benz. If you get easy-to-use, leak-free faucets, simply using water will make you happy. Put a kitchen counter in the middle of the room with a small sink and a high-arc faucet; it will completely change your life. You can fill a vase from the table, and make flower arranging more fun.

Booklovers can make walls out of bookcases, collect books like a library does, and live in a maze of books. Surrounded by handpicked books, you can read comfortably to your heart's content. Those who love the outdoors, returning home mostly just to sleep, should place relative importance on the bedroom, carefully testing mattresses or futons for maximum sleep quality. It might also be interesting to set up a big high-quality screen and sound system like in a theater, for bedside viewing.

In cities, we rely on urban amenities in our daily lives. For people who eat out most of the time, it would be amusing to condense the faucet, sink, and refrigerator into a sideboard next to the sofa. You could make tea while sitting on the sofa, or make a highball while watching TV, using ice balls from a small freezer.

I've jotted these ideas down as they came to mind, but if every person thought about the center of his or her own lifestyle, the shapes of our homes would naturally take on greater variety. But I've never seen anything like most of these homes. Most people live in houses like all the other houses. There are unexplored possibilities here.

Among my architect and designer friends, hardly any have built and live in a detached home in Tokyo. They either renovated an old building or they rent. It's not that they don't make much money. It's a natural choice. Single-story houses are comfortable, but in an overcrowded city like Tokyo, they're either too expensive or you can't find suitable land, even if you have the capital. The overwhelming majority of spacious floor plans are found in condominiums. However, when it comes to renovating something to suit yourself, since you would of course hesitate to tear down a brand-new building, you end up looking for something suitable in existing structures. Moreover, you're more likely

to find a nice quiet place to live in long-established residential areas rich with greenery than in an inhospitable environment bristling with high-rise complexes.

"Expanding domestic demand" has become a kind of catchphrase, but it makes sense to look for some real demand in people's daily lives. It's nonsense to lay more roads or build more dams. Everyone already has a car. And because we're in a recession, no one feels like traveling abroad. But what if most people realized that they could rationally renovate their homes? We have the highest accumulated savings deposits in the world. The key to revitalizing domestic demand is to get them to release those savings into circulation. If the infill of existing structures were gradually turned over like snacks on a grill, continually renewing the interiors, it would generate a huge expansion in domestic demand.

It's true that we are experiencing a rapid aging of the population, but older people have accumulated more savings than younger people. It would be good if discriminating adults with rich life experiences could renovate "end-of-life homes." Although signs of this tendency are visible, demand in Japan's housing market is still slack, probably reflecting the stagnant global economy. To accelerate movement in this direction, we need both institutional and creative support. Because design is a business of conception, it can help by materializing the latent possibilities.

The Abundance of Non-possession

To make a living space beautiful, we must rid it of as many objects as possible. At some point, we began to believe that owning things made us rich. During the period of rapid economic growth, the Three Sacred Treasures (the Japanese imperial regalia consisting of the mirror, the sword, and the crescent jewel) became the television, refrigerator, and washing machine (and later, the car, air conditioner, and color TV). Perhaps before they knew it, postwar Japanese, formerly starving, eagerly pursued a sense of fulfillment by acquiring things. But it turns out that an overabundance of things does not bring us comfort. We actually feel better when we pare things down to the bare minimum. The simplicity of non-possession breeds spirituality and a rich imagination; this has been the Japanese philosophy throughout history.

The Dojinsai study at Jishoji temple and Katsura Imperial Villa are so refreshing because they are completely empty. If they overflowed with all sorts of miscellaneous items and furnishings, it would be too terrible to look at. These sophisticated spaces were arranged simply, and when they were used for living, there were only a few furnishings, which were carefully used and then stored. Things that are not in use, no matter how splendid they may be, should be stored away. This is the Japanese way.

However, if we were to tear the roofs off of contemporary Japanese houses for a bird's-eye view, most would be overflowing with stuff, because we rushed headlong into ownership and continue to this day. We are like a greedy rabbit who once suffered from hunger; he is anxious unless he is holding a biscuit with both paws. Considering this objectively, it's clear that his life would be easier if he had nothing in his paws; he would be able to greet someone with a handshake or arrange flowers.

Material World, a book by photographer Peter Menzel, features portraits of families in various cultures, with all of their household goods lined up in front of their houses. I don't recall how many families, cultures, or countries he included, but I do remember clearly that the Japanese family's household items were striking in their multitude. I stared at the photo in dumb amazement, wondering when on earth Japanese began to live surrounded by so much stuff. It was astonishing how skillfully and carefully they had assembled so many not completely useless, but surely unnecessary objects. These photographs, quietly exposing the downside of consumption, suggested that somewhere we took the wrong path.

Each and every object involves production and marketing. Objects are planned, modified, implemented, and take shape in the world through a far-reaching course of manufacturing that has its origins in the extraction of natural resources like petroleum or iron. Then advertising and promotion, supported by distribution, push these goods into people's lives. How much energy does this consume? And what if most products are messy, inconsistent, and unnecessary? If most of the resources, imagination, transportation, radio waves, advertising pamphlets, and commercials expended effect no result other than contaminating our lives, then nothing could be more futile.

Perhaps we've unconsciously become overly tolerant of a Japan overflowing with things. It may be a result of internalizing our pride in the postwar GDP, second in the world; or maybe the craving for material goods in the immediate postwar era confounded the scale by which we sense happiness. The spectacular oversupply of goods available in the electronics district of Akihabara or any high-end brand shop might seem comfortingly dependable to anyone who has experienced a fervent desire for things. So before realizing it, the Japanese people were over-buying and became insensitive to its abnormality.

We should be prepared to throw things out. We shouldn't see this as *mottainai* (regrettably wasteful, almost sacrilegious). Of course I can sympathize with the feeling that discarding something is *mottainai*, because we were enchanted with it at one time, but if the sense of *mottainai* functions only at the point when we are finally throwing away what is already an enormous amount of waste, it may not be perceptive enough. At that point, it's too late. You should feel it when something is being mass-produced, or later, when you're buying it. It is not jettisoning the object that is *mottainai,* but rather the series of efforts conceived and executed with the goal of manufacturing a useless object destined for disposal.

We should be more critical of mass production. We should not take foolish pride in industrial output. Mass production and mass consumption are not simply the result of industry's selfish desire to expand. Also complicit is the poverty of the consumer's imagination, which cannot envision the end of consumption. There's nothing wrong with selling something, as long as it will make the world more pleasant or comfortable, and it's only natural for people to desire such things. But it is in no way pleasant or comfortable to hoard things that aren't even useful.

When I stay at a high-quality *ryokan*, I feel my sensitivity rise several degrees. This is because both mind and body can relax, since scrupulous attention is paid to the space. The standard for arrangement and accessories is the distribution of a minimal number of objects. Precisely because there are very few things in the room, my eyes are drawn to the beauty of the woven surface of the tatami mats, and I am enticed by the appearance of the plaster of the walls. My eyes turn to the flowers arranged in a vase in the alcove, and I am able to fully enjoy the beauty of the dishes on which the meal is arrayed. My conscious mind spontaneously opens up to the natural world represented in the garden. It's the same in a hotel. Precisely because it is a highly simplified environment, a guest can become aware of the material of which a towel is made and the softness of a bathrobe that evokes the delicate sensitivity of the skin.

This applies to ordinary residences as well. If you were to limit the objects in a modern home to the bare minimum, disposing of useless items, the living space would certainly become more comfortable. As an experiment, try removing most of the things cluttering your living space. An unexpectedly beautiful space is likely to appear.

To discard unnecessary things and live simply is to make a background for savoring and experiencing your implements of living. There is an appropriate beauty to all tools, instruments, and utensils, even if they are not works of art. Even a very ordinary glass, when you put some ice in it and pour whisky over it, is suffused with a delightful amber color. A frosted glass becomes even more appealing the moment it is set carefully upon an elegant coaster on an immaculate table. On the other hand, even if there is a piece of beguiling jet black lacquerware prepared to be exhibited in praise of shadows, it is difficult for one to savor its elegance in a dining room overflowing with stuff, with remote controls and other objects scattered about.

There are scenes and experiences that make me feel very fortunate to have been born in Japan: A single sheet of white paper placed on an unvarnished wooden counter; a small bowl of celadon porcelain placed neatly on a lacquer tray; the aroma wafting from a lacquer bowl of broth the moment you lift the lid. Some may say that people don't want that transcendent tension in their ordinary everyday lives. Indeed, some think that loosening and openness, not tension, give us a sense of comfort. Home is also a place of relaxation. But the idea that unlimited allowance for indulgence leads to relaxation is misguided. When we use things, when there is just the slightest space or setting for their latent beauty to be manifested, we are filled with the joy of living. This has always given people a sense of satisfaction.

There have been many attempts to revitalize traditional handicrafts, redesigning them to fit today's lifestyles, or proposing new uses for them. I have been involved in such efforts myself. Whether it was lacquerware or porcelain, I felt that the crux of the problem was not how alluring an object we could create, but how we could resuscitate a lifestyle in which we could gracefully appreciate such objects. The reason lacquerware doesn't sell isn't that it has lost its popularity. Even today, when people see fine lacquerware, they are deeply impressed. However, the margins and empty spaces in which one can appreciate and enjoy it are gradually being lost.

This applies to contemporary products as well. What is important is not the number of one's possessions or the degree of their splendor, but the depth of their use. Without a place where an object is used well or completely, neither the object nor the richness of everyday life with which it is entrusted can attain full realization. That's why we have to act now to change the form of the home for the future. Things that grow and develop change shape. The home is the same.

The first step is to get rid of things. This should be done with a sense of taking the *mottainai* spirit to a new level. We must free ourselves from an existence as people of a country who own more meaningless household goods than any other, and return to an existence as people of a country with a delicate sensitivity that creates everyday living spaces in which the charms of an object can blossom against a backdrop of simplicity. Place a chopstick rest on an empty table. Then, precisely place a pair of chopsticks on it. Already you're living an enriched life.

Exporting the Japanese Home

You might doubt that people around the world could possibly be interested in our cramped and uniform housing. Anything is possible. A lifestyle in which one removes his or her shoes at the entrance, facilitating direct contact and interaction between the body and the environmental interface, holds great possibility for the future. As people are encouraged to remake living spaces to match their lifestyles, I can anticipate the emergence of unique living environments that are hybrids of Japanese tradition and high technology.

Japan has established its position as an industrial superpower by manufacturing and exporting a great variety of industrial goods. What we're going to export next to East Asia is not refrigerators or air conditioners, 3D TVs or smartphones. If the house itself is conceived as a high-tech appliance, a product integrating living space and advanced technology, Japan is positioned advantageously to explore its possibilities. Homes are already beginning to be controlled by technology; we will see more of this in the future.

All advanced nations are working to promote research on the efficient use of renewable energy. Technology is quickly evolving toward testing just how efficiently we can extract, manage, store, and distribute energy, whether it be solar, wind, geothermal, or biomass. From early on, Japan has been working on systems like photovoltaic power generation and cogeneration that recycle surplus energy into heat. Research on passive houses that skillfully harvest and apply natural energy is now moving toward practical application. Japan also leads the world in technologies for electric cars and storage batteries. Our electric supply system, controlled by telecommunications, is resistant to problems like power outages. We can expect to stand at the forefront of the field of technology-controlled homes as well. Japan has been thrown into a difficult situation by the Tohoku earthquake, but we should see this as an opportunity to make great strides in developing technology for alternative energy and the environment.

High-tech changes in the home are proceeding at an accelerated rate. Home theaters went through an ostentatious phase, with tower speakers proliferating like mushrooms, but soon the entire living space will be transformed into a complete sound stage in which it will be impossible to tell where the speakers are. Televisions, now huge, flat monitors hung on the wall, will likely soon be installed into the wall. Or perhaps they will assert their existence as objects even more. Either way, today's TVs, whose shape is in limbo, will probably cease to exist. Lighting will become part of the ceilings, televisions and communications equipment will become part of the walls, and the environment will quietly begin to develop a rapport with people and the human body.

What if floors were equipped with delicate sensors? The lifestyle in which you take off your shoes before stepping up into the room means that the floor – that is, the environmental interface – and the human body can interact directly. The human body is a mass of information. If the physiological data (blood pressure, pulse, weight, temperature, and so on) could be detected, a dialogue between the body and the environment could begin through the floor, and people might conduct intentional communication through the medium of the residence. Because electrically conductive fibers have already been developed, the need for physical switches and keyboards is fading. What if these advanced conductive fibers became a carpet with internal sensors? Since most hospital exams record physiological data, people's bodies could be connected with hospitals through the home and be continuously monitored by medical services. Setting aside issues of morality and privacy, it might be possible to collect health information through remote methods other than phone or email. This is in no way an absurd idea.

Of course, even without going that far into the future, through high technology, Japan is already at the forefront of a clear trend towards the rebirth of the home as an advanced consumer electronics product, with systems for lighting, the kitchen, bath temperature control, and HVAC. Japan lags behind the U.S. in the development of computer operating systems and search engines, but making the home more intelligent – adapting technology to everyday space – is our area of expertise. If we could hold a home show instead of a car show – one loaded with information presenting a variety of tangible examples that made use of new technology for the home – users with a mature level of desire would enthusiastically respond to and welcome it. Japan has many talented architects and designers who could actually work to make it happen.

Furthermore, if we establish a structure which, through ever more active social media, sought to keep a close eye on these activities, one could quickly get all the information one needed and easily obtain responses to one's individual consultations, and progress relatively smoothly toward harvesting the fruit of a new home.

Recently, I've learned that the know-how of a semi-public institution, the Urban Renaissance Agency, will be employed in China. The URA was formerly known as the Japan Housing Corporation (founded in 1955). Its initial role of supplying residences to mid-level employees during Japan's period of high economic growth has ended, and its focus has been transferred to refabricating existing apartment complexes into higher-quality residences and ensuring a stable supply of homes for senior citizens with declining incomes. It's unfortunate, but such are the issues facing our nation. However, the URA's housing project is surprisingly interesting. Using the term "architectural reduction," the project proposes spacious plans created by eliminating walls or ceilings, perpendicularly or horizontally, providing new roof terraces by eliminating higher floors, adding elevators to buildings that previously only had stairs, and so forth. Advanced construction methods are being used to renovate old apartment houses. Moreover, as the result of accumulated research in this field, there is such an abundance of detail in the renovations that it is hard to believe that these were former public housing units.

These include the superb placement of communal amenities; improvements to make building maintenance easier, like externalizing piping; and the creation of a skyline that is intriguing rather than monotonous by installing sloped roofs that accent the surrounding landscape. Although the URA has been criticized as a place where retired government officials land, in fact the agency has been doing good work.

China, on the other hand, is compelled by explosive urbanization to find a way to accelerate the provision of residential housing. Though China's wealthy are frequently discussed, the income of an average Chinese worker is one tenth that of his or her Japanese counterpart. These rank-and-file workers anticipating higher incomes comprise the reality of China as a superpower of the future. Where will the Chinese government find an effective precedent? In Japan, of course. Within the Tokyo metropolitan area alone, the URA has successfully supplied and managed nearly a thousand apartment complexes for more than 400,000 households.

When Premier Wen Jiabao of China visited Japan, he mentioned that China had great expectations for Japan's environmental technology. I don't think he was just being diplomatic. A healthy urban environment requires the development of rigorous infrastructure. Japan will probably be able to help with the practical aspects of creating a proper energy supply system for rapid urbanization, mechanisms for waste disposal and resource recycling, and residential construction and city planning.

In many Chinese cities, including Beijing and Shanghai,

foreign architects hold exhibitions presenting various development plans premised on China's rapid urbanization. I have seen some, and every one of them pursues preposterous, slightly fanciful plans that assume an astoundingly broad scale of development. Only in Japan will you find an example of the actual supply of residential units to hundreds of thousands of individuals. If we consider these achievements and build on that experience and insight, incorporating cutting-edge and environmental technologies into a vision for solid and practical development, we can cooperate with this vast neighboring country in its robust urban growth.

The Japanese are beginning to lean toward lifestyle-appropriate housing. Meanwhile, the household environment in which one removes footwear before entering seems poised to deliver a new interactivity between the body and the environment. Moreover, we can provide sound, reliable consultation on large-scale city planning in both hardware and software. Herein lies the possibility for us to lead Asian lifestyle culture via the Japanese idea of "home."

If we're serious about approaching the rest of Asia, we should probably know that in India, people also remove their footwear before entering a home.

Chapter 4

Tourism: Cultural DNA

How to Brand Japan

No country in the world compares to Japan when it comes to service. Japanese inns and restaurants reflect the nation's unique hospitality and haute cuisine culture, with prices comparable or higher than Western-style luxury hotels. High-quality service can be found in India and China, but it's not consistent, as the service is at a traditional inn (*ryokan*) in Japan. There is a formal aspect to *ryokan* hospitality, but it is still deeply popular not only among Japanese people, but also with visitors from overseas. Looking objectively at the broad appeal of these forms of hospitality rooted in our culture, we can begin to see the evolving shape of tourism and imagine how it will support the future of Japanese industry.

Katsura Rikyu is an imperial villa on the outskirts of Kyoto. It has been described as an index of how Japan confronts as well as converges with the West. It seems to possess a singular aesthetic positioned at the intersection of local and global values. Understanding that singularity will help us to understand the unique potential of Japan's aesthetic resources.

Katsura Rikyu was built as a villa for the Hachijo no Miya branch of the imperial family in the seventeenth century. Its architecture was based on adding to the established *shoin-zukuri* style elements of the *sukiya-zukuri* style, grounded in tea-house aesthetics. This exquisite architecture holds a special place in Japanese hearts as a standard of traditional beauty in its deft balance of serenity and surprise. It works with the aesthetic of simplicity developed by the samurai class to arrive at the elegance – the almost weightless refinement – of the imperial aristocracy. And from a modernist perspective it has attracted continuous interest from overseas connoisseurs as an outstanding aesthetic landmark. However, my focus here is not on its architectural design but on the villa as a subject for photography and photography books.

Katsura Rikyu, a collection of photographs by Yasuhiro Ishimoto, was published in the spring of 2010. It was his fourth published collection featuring the imperial villa. The 2010 collection includes monochrome prints taken in 1954 and color prints taken in 1981, so some were taken almost sixty years ago and even the latest ones are from about thirty years ago. The photographer's brilliant point of view is still present in these photographs, despite the lapse of time. The story of how these photographs were taken, how they were laid out, and how they were made into a book is rich in implications regarding the perceptual awakening that took place in the contact between Katsura Rikyu – and by extension, the traditional Japanese aesthetic – and Western modernism.

Ishimoto's first collection was published in 1960, probably in connection with the World Design Conference in Tokyo. Design and layout were by Herbert Bayer, who studied and taught at the Bauhaus. The Japanese architect Kenzo Tange and Walter Gropius, founder of the Bauhaus, contributed essays. Tange, the principal editor, seems to have intended to employ the clear vision of Western modernism to evoke the universality of Japanese aesthetics. The book's layout is distinctive and subtle, with a resonance between the photographs, boldly cropped vertically and horizontally, and ample margins. In an exterior photo of the *shoin*, for example, traditional wood-shingled roofs are intrepidly cropped to conspicuously present a precisely composed grid-like order that recalls a Mondrian painting. In other words, Katsura Rikyu is treated here as a modernist ideal discovered in Japan.

The second book was what might be called a revised edition, published in 1971 with a modified layout by Yusaku Kamekura and with Kenzo Tange as sole contributing writer. Here we can sense in the layout and book design a Japanese-style revision of the previous edition's straightforward Western perspective. While the first edition begins with the *katsuragaki* bamboo fence that surrounds Katsura Rikyu and ends with the handle of the *fusuma* sliding door, the second edition begins and ends with a grove of bamboo. In an interview with the architect Hiroshi Naito in 2008, Ishimoto revealed that these photographs of bamboo in the second edition were actually taken in the Sagano district of Kyoto – not at Katsura Rikyu.

The third book is in color, featuring photographs taken in 1981 that capture the interior of the villa after a large-scale restoration. An interpretive essay by the architect Arata Isozaki aims to restore an overview of Katsura Rikyu, which was somewhat abstracted in the second edition. The layout almost completely rejects cropping, making full use of the proportions of the original large-format photographs. With the soft appearance of greenery, of moss and trees, abstractness recedes in favor of a

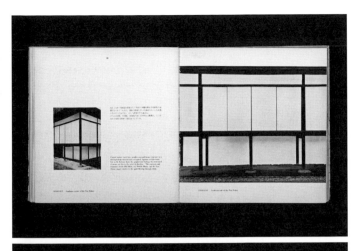

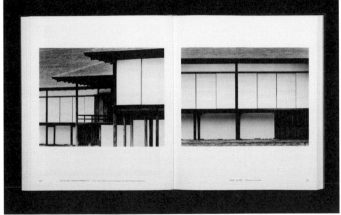

Above: *Katsura: Tradition and Creation in Japanese Architecture*, published in 1960; designed by Herbert Bayer
Below: *Katsura Rikyu*, published in 2010; book design by Ikko Tanaka and layout by Tetsuya Ohta

natural, gentle appearance. Book design was by Ikko Tanaka, with layout by Tetsuya Ohta.

The fourth edition is a reprint, mainly featuring the monochrome photographs from the first edition. Tetsuya Ohta handled both book design and layout. Hiroshi Naito wrote the preface. Rejecting Bayer's bold first-edition cropping, these images, respecting the originals, convey their vigor and give me goosebumps.

A variety of ways to identify Japan through Katsura Rikyu becomes apparent, as reflected through the eyes of Yasuhiro Ishimoto. Born in San Francisco, Yasuhiro Ishimoto moved to Japan with his parents when he was three; he lived in Kochi prefecture until he graduated from high school. Subsequently, he returned to the United States alone, spending World War II in an internment camp in Colorado as a second-generation Japanese-American. There he became interested in photography and eventually studied it in earnest in Chicago. Some of the first art books he bought were Laszlo Moholy-Nagy's *Vision in Motion* and György Kepes's *Language of Vision*, both pioneering experimental visual design studies to which Ishimoto's inborn talent predisposed him; he enrolled in the photography department of the Chicago Institute of Design, known as the New Bauhaus, established by Moholy-Nagy after he emigrated to the United States. Building a foundation for himself at the New Bauhaus as a photographer looking at the world from a compositional perspective, Ishimoto graduated in 1953. Upon the death of Moholy-Nagy, the New Bauhaus merged with the

Illinois Institute of Technology, which itself was an educational institution founded by Ludwig Mies van der Rohe, the architect who served as the last director of the Bauhaus. So Ishimoto became a photographer schooled in modernism through a direct line from the Bauhaus.

After graduating, Ishimoto returned to Japan and started his photography career. Someone encouraged him to begin photographing Katsura Rikyu, which in Ishimoto's eyes overlapped with Mies's glass-and-steel apartment towers on Chicago's Lake Shore Drive. He had the insight to see the structural composition of the villa in terms of the curtain walls of modernist architecture that he used in his student days as a subject for practicing the swing, tilt, and shift adjustments on his view camera. But a Japanese sensibility also percolates beneath his insight. It was here that he developed a perspective on the shape of things to come: an eye that could see Japan through Western modernism. Ishimoto is blessed with this eye, and the Katsura Rikyu captured in his early monochrome photographs reflects it.

The Katsura Rikyu in his photographs appears much more sublime than the actual villa, compositionally featuring an elegant order like a rhythmical mathematical series hidden in the configuration of Japanese-style rooms. The purity and concision captured in these photographs resonates so remarkably with modernism that it is as if modernism itself had been anticipated in early Edo Japan. The actual villa has far more stylistic incongruities. In this sense, the images from Ishimoto's second series are complementary to these earlier photographs.

A mode of thought that both relativized and connected the Japanese tradition with Western modernism was distinctly displayed through the medium of Ishimoto's photographs of Katsura Rikyu. This is why this series of photography books has been repeatedly updated and continues to serve as a benchmark for images of Katsura Rikyu, even after all these years.

Essentially, Japanese culture has been considered distinctively different from that of modern European countries. The ruling class of samurai wore their hair in topknots and carried swords at the waist, dressed in *kamishimo* (jumper-like garments with extended shoulders) and pleated culottes called *hakama*. Their footwear consisted of thonged sandals or wooden clogs called *geta*, and they relaxed on *zabuton* cushions on tatami mats. Some three hundred years before Europe modernized, a national style evolved in Japan through the invention of techniques that encouraged free use of the imagination by applying an extreme minimalism grounded in simplicity. This produced a variety of art practices, such as the tea ceremony, ikebana, landscape gardening, *renga* collaborative poetry, architecture, furniture, Noh theater, and *buyo* dance. Three hundred years of self-imposed isolation during the Edo period contributed to the increasing maturity and refinement of these practices, cultural uniqueness so pronounced that our self-consciousness around it has sometimes befuddled us. The Netherlands, Spain, England, United States, and France each have their own originality, but compared to Japan, their similarities would seem to outweigh their differences.

Consequently, when Japan confronted Western modernity

after the Meiji Restoration, it wasn't easy to maintain our nation's distinctive culture. Undeniably, we were driven by impatience to participate in the progress of civilization, immediately shedding our traditional dress, exchanging sandals for shoes, and replacing topknots with short hair. But over time there was a backlash. The cultural DNA embedded deep in our sensibilities is tenacious.

As the novelist Jun'ichiro Tanizaki wrote in his essay *In Praise of Shadows* (1933), ever since the Meiji Restoration we Japanese have guiltily suspected that we might have created an entirely different type of modern life if we had imported only technology and not allowed Westernization to infiltrate the culture. This guilt-ridden journey follows the trajectory of Japan's cultural modernization, which has been punctuated from time to time by the various editions of Ishimoto's *Katsura Rikyu*. Ishimoto's photographs reveal Katsura Rikyu's inherent universality from a perspective that intuitively grasps the continuity between Western modernism and Japanese culture. The early monochrome photographs in particular distill Japanese culture into a form that shines all the more brilliantly in a global context. The successive editions of Ishimoto's photographs are evidence that, to this day, his perspective remains tremendously inspiring.

Once upon a time, Japanese enjoyed viewing the moon from a veranda called a *tsukimidai*. Today, we can share in that beauty through photographs of a *tsukimidai*. Aesthetics can be reborn even through the eye of a needle.

The View from a Compound Eye

I had the chance to visit one of the newly built Aman resorts, the hotel Amanfayun in Hangzhou, China. Hangzhou was once the capital of the Southern Song dynasty (1127–1279), one of the most artistically and culturally refined periods in Chinese history. Even today, we can sense the lingering essence of that prosperity. The expansive landscape of West Lake is reminiscent of an ink-wash painting, an art form that reached its peak during the Southern Song dynasty. In the early morning, the slowly moving, fluid forms of elderly Tai Chi practitioners on the lakeside melt into the misty haze. The resort's elegant architecture ingeniously incorporating the scenery of the lake, the tranquility of the white porcelain table settings, and the occasionally glimpsed pieces of elegant calligraphy all serve to recall the Chinese literati tradition.

Here, on the outskirts of the city, we find ourselves in an exclusive resort that recalls a tea plantation village of the distant past. The 14-hectare site is covered with dense greenery, including tea gardens and bamboo groves. There are forty-two unique structures, each a recreation of a traditional Chinese home. Unobtrusively equipped with modern conveniences such as high-speed Internet, TV, and sound systems, the villas and suites are furnished in a traditional Chinese style tailored to ensure modern comfort. The "spa zone," located in a row of traditional houses, offers treatments based on traditional Chinese medicine. In the tea rooms, built centuries ago, you can enjoy a variety of teas, including the local high-quality Longjing, served with classic teaware in a traditional atmosphere. Stylish bamboo bird cages are arranged here and there, the warble of birds blending from time to time with the sound of the wind in the trees. In the morning, vapor from the steamer rises from the restaurant kitchen and disappears into the sky. The magnificent grounds are interconnected with paths of carefully laid paving stones, creating a soothing atmosphere for your stroll. This is Amanfayun. The way the topography, tradition, fixtures, furnishings, and etiquette of this ancient capital of China were adopted as resources for the hospitality of the hotel made me aware of the skill of Aman-style management.

If the Japanese aesthetic is a resource for our future, how do we leverage it in the tourism industry? The Aman Resorts hotel group, created by Adrian Zecha, an Indonesian who grew up in Singapore, provides us with one point of reference. While grounded in a Western approach to operations, Aman has an original philosophy that negates this logic, inventing a new trend in the thinking about resort hotels with the concept of a sort of "anti-hotel." This distinctive approach conceptualizes and manages the hotel as an ideal harvest of the local culture, carefully utilizing the scenery, topography, climate, traditions, and styles of the region in which the hotel is situated.

Aman Resorts' first hotel, Amanpuri, was built in 1988 on Thailand's Phuket Island. Today, the group is expanding and includes twenty-four small-scale hotels, in Bhutan, Cambodia, France, French Polynesia, Indonesia, India, Morocco, the Philippines, Sri Lanka, Thailand, Turks and Caicos, United States, and China. The word "Aman" means peace in Sanskrit, and is included in the names of all of the hotels, followed by a short word incorporating the hotel's unique theme. The first hotel, Amanpuri, means "place of peace." All of the guest rooms are independent villas, and while there are fewer than fifty rooms, a large number of staff is assigned to each.

The management of exclusive resort hotels is like that of wineries; art and business meet in seeking to realize a utopian vision while maintaining profitability. It's an extremely tricky gamble of sensibility, like threading the eye of a needle; it requires a string of skillful moves by an expert in both economics and aesthetics. Success depends on two points: first, whether you can present to customers, moment to moment, a joy and satisfaction transcending the everyday in all aspects of their resort experience; and second, whether customers will gladly pay a price for that experience corresponding to your investment. It's essential to build on customer excitement at contact with a unique culture and tantalizing natural environment, but we might take a step further and say that the essence of this business is the education of desire – transforming customer expectations of the resort experience through services that accelerate and deepen curiosity about a foreign country and culture.

Following a long period of overseas exploration and colonial expansion that dated back to the late fifteenth century, Westerners sought to enjoy exquisite residences and food in places far from civilization. In the Sahara Desert or South America's

Amazon River basin, or Maasai Mara in Kenya, teeming with wild animals, they dined on the finest European cuisine at tables covered with white tablecloths, with formally dressed waiters pouring their wine – luxury bordering on arrogance – a practice that expanded along with their cultural predominance. But people are no longer impressed by resorts that import Western culture into remote places. This is because there is a growing number of people who are finely attuned to the endless combinations of cultural diversity our planet has to offer.

Adrian Zecha, who once worked as a Far East regional manager for *Life* and *Time* magazines, has personally incorporated into his business sense the tastes and lifestyles of the world's wealthy. This is why he was so perceptive regarding the limits of learning from the West and the possibilities of Asian culture. The quality of these resorts is not encapsulated in their architecture or interior design. Of course, these elements are significant, but the crucial point lies elsewhere – in "experience design," the fabric of hospitality that interweaves the varied layers of every moment, every instant of the stay.

If a hotel's reputation is the client's first point of contact, then experience design begins there. Aman Resorts does not advertise. Future clients get their information from impressions conveyed by former guests or careful coverage in magazines and such. The organization's websites are minimal, providing a very small window opening momentarily via the Internet. Guests who have been enticed by word-of-mouth reports and other information in amounts small enough to leave room for their imaginations to fill out the image arrive at the hotel entrance with their hearts bursting with anticipation. By this point, experience design has already been activated.

What is the appearance and demeanor of staff members who greet the guests? Where are guests taken, and on what kind of furniture will they sit? In what kind of glass will drinks be brought to them, at what interval will they be served, what sort of anticipation will be created? What will the atmosphere of check-in be like, and what sort of forms and information will guests fill out, with what kind of pen? What type of room key and key holder will guests be given before being led to their room? There are countless subtle experiences woven into even the short interval between guests entering the resort and opening the door to their room. Eventually, passing through the scrupulously kept gardens on stone footpaths, the guest arrives at his or her own villa, but naturally, in this journey as well, there are innumerable nodes of experience. In the room, the guest will probably take a breath, slowly open the closet door, take off his coat, and put it on a hanger. Or she might get a chilled drink from the refrigerator, pour it in the tumbler provided and take a sip. Something that works every second must be carefully organized in advance. The moment the guest touches the hanger, the instant she opens the refrigerator, the minute she looks for the corkscrew, and the twinkling of an eye in which she glances at the coaster under the tumbler are all opportunities for hospitality.

The magnificent architecture incorporating the environment, the view from the quiet pool merging with the scenery, the dazzling feast, the pleasure of the spa – all of these will be deeply imprinted in the hearts of the guests, an unforgettable impression built on multiple layers of meticulous service.

To arrange flowers is to have the mind attend to a space. A space does not mean a volume defined by walls, but an area where consciousness brings the bright light of attention into play. When a single stone is placed on an otherwise empty tabletop, it creates a particular tension. Through the medium of this tension, one's awareness is suddenly drawn to this "space." As if lit candles were placed one by one in the surroundings, the conscious mind, gradually illuminated, creates a space within. To arrange flowers is this kind of activity. While one is shaping the arrangement, it is mindfulness that animates the space.

If you observe Aman Resorts closely, you can sense Japan in the background. Zecha, who has stayed in Kyoto, says that he was influenced by *ryokan*. But the hospitality performed in top-tier Japanese *ryokan* takes a different form in Aman – not only in the way flowers are arranged, but also in the timing of service, the techniques of using the garden and water to incorporate nature, and so forth. Visitors can sense these differences.

Aman Resorts has expanded to the point of having twenty-four hotels around the world, but the total number of accommodations is a fraction of that of a single large-scale resort hotel in Las Vegas. That's how carefully their experience design is laid out. More than once, Japan's culture has been rediscovered by cosmopolitans who have wished to capitalize on it in a global context. Zecha is one of them. Having graduated from its status

A footpath leading to the villas retains the charm of the Longjing tea village;
Amanfayun resort in Hangzhou, China

as an industrialized nation, Japan must shift its commercial
activities to the value-added field of tourism. Aman Resorts can
be seen as a precedent.

The times are now rapidly moving toward the rise of
Asia. The percentage of Asian clients supporting the resort industry is predicted to rise gradually. Unlike Europeans, Asians do
not take long holidays. Their enjoyment of nature is also different. In these new circumstances, how can we shape their desire
for future resort hotels?

A room featuring a *hakuji* white porcelain vase offers a seamless integration with the local aesthetic culture; Amanfayun resort in Hangzhou, China

For a long time, as the only industrialized nation in Asia, Japan followed its own path, but now we need compound eyes to re-evaluate our value in light of the rise and economic vitality of other Asian nations. We need hotels so highly rated that people around the world will be inspired to ask their friends if they've visited.

Conceiving an Asian-style Resort

The root of "resort" means to go frequently, but now it also denotes recuperation or sightseeing. The concept is derived from an image of the essence of pleasure, continuously attracting people. It's a word that appears when society becomes just a bit affluent, and you might also describe it as a form of relaxation offering a kind of refreshment that you would like to experience again and again. Once when I was talking with the Hong Kong designer Alan Chan, I said that I would list "rest" after the first three necessities of life – food, clothing, and shelter – and he said "travel." For people living in crowded Hong Kong, there is a latent desire to break away and fly off to any place they like. In contrast, people in Japan are often seeking rest, having run non-stop since the rapid growth of the economy. Whether it means rest or travel, "resort" follows the first three necessities, and so design, which controls disparity and educates desire, cannot overlook it, because it probably constitutes a huge latent value and economic resource.

What is a resort, to Asians? As I mentioned above, Westerners who traveled the world have reproduced their own lifestyle within foreign cultures and in natural environments far from civilization, exhibiting a great desire to enjoy these experiences. For instance, in the town of Manaus in the Amazon River basin, which flourished as a distribution center for natural rubber, there still stands an abandoned opera house. You can feel the vestiges of the energy of the desire to expend tremendous money, time, and effort to realize a dream in a foreign country. This is also true of African safaris. Apparently *safari* means journey in Swahili, but in English, it always includes hunting. It was Westerners who brought guns to the African continent, fired them riotously at the abundant wild game, and, gazing at nearby giraffes and rhinos, enjoyed the finest food and wine with white tablecloths and waiters in uniform.

It seems that for a long time there has been an undercurrent of euphoria over this debauchery and pleasure in the value system surrounding resorts, which would be regarded as immoral or unethical by today's standards. It was a macho view of the concept of resort: not simply recuperation or recreation, it took the shape of the desires of the powerful. Risk-taking is essential in the process of building wealth and realizing a dream. They might have felt exhausted and depleted, after exposure to such jeopardy. This is why dissipation and decadence are seen at the resorts of the powerful. Perhaps it's an ecstasy akin to stomping on the accelerator when one is headed toward destruction. The resorts that blossomed in remote places are the relics of such Western desires. If we are to consider resorts from an Asian perspective, we mustn't simply imitate the veneer of Western resorts.

Nevertheless, today's resort hotels are homogenous. At the beginning of *Anna Karenina*, Tolstoy wrote, "All happy families are alike; each unhappy family is unhappy in its own way." I wonder if the sense of security that comes from adhering to established forms is linked to ease and pleasure. Shining sun. A sofa with a parasol by a spacious pool. Palm trees and whitecaps. A restaurant on a hill overlooking a superb view. Western food with an ethnic touch. Within the extraordinary, there is a safe track leading to peace of mind and relaxation.

The Hawaiian Islands, Tahiti, Bali, Phuket, the Canary Islands, the Seychelles, Mozambique – all of these islands are bathed by the sun, tickled by light breezes, and basking in comfortable water and atmosphere. These are the kinds of places where many luxury resorts have been built. Each has a unique culture and history. Some have been marked by friction with colonialism or unique conflicts, including civil war. But negative issues are cleanly swept away in the marketing images and services offered.

Americans took over the Kingdom of Hawaii in the nineteenth century, disenfranchising the native people. But when you arrive there, you forget that history. If you listen to the music of the place, the ukulele and the slide guitar, or open yourself to the movements of the hula, your heart is soothed. The reverberant sound of the Hawaiian language – especially the nouns – seems to relax the senses. Exposed to their spell-like inflections – *ala moana*, *halekulani*, *hula*, *lomilomi* – along with the Hawaiian melodies, you feel as if body and soul might melt away, together with all your accumulated fatigue. Just as people have natural gifts, there are gifted places on earth; I believe that Hawaii is full of a natural healing spirit.

In Bali, the unique island culture called Balinese Hinduism is seasoned with an admixture of Dutch culture that functions as a spice, slightly bracing an atmosphere that tends to be dominated by relaxation and a sense of openness or freedom. This place – where if you listen, you can hear almost anywhere the sound of the gamelan – has somehow managed to preserve its dignity as an island of the gods. Yet it must be said that the countless hotels built here are largely homogeneous in concept. Entrances and lobbies employ Balinese-style architecture. Whether near the sea or the mountains, an infinity pool is sited toward the most intense scenery, beautifully incorporating the landscape. The many villas skillfully utilizing the topography of the place are splendid, but the underlying sensibility of the resort is unmistakably Western.

Perhaps sticking to type is a shortcut to comfort, but what if we free ourselves from the conventional colonial-style resort and imagine what an Asian-style resort would look like? And why not in Indonesia? Indonesia is a country made up of 18,000 separate islands, stretching east to west across an area equivalent to the continental United States. What if one of these islands were operated as a huge botanical garden, not with rows of greenhouses and geodesic domes, but a botanical garden in which native plants are grown with as little interference as possible?

Here you do not admire flowers, but appreciate the plants themselves – not their rarity or scarcity, but the luxurious growth of vegetation. Imagine, on one of these islands, luffa sponge gourds grow large, mangos droop with the weight of their fruit, and a multitude of plants spread their leaves in their native landscape. We would feel ourselves absorbing life energy from these

Terrace view and luxuriant greenery from House of Kedewatan in Ubud, Bali

surroundings. You might say this creates a resonance between the power of plants and the rejuvenating power that is at the root of human life. This is a place for enjoying a rapport with the life force hidden within plants, rather than the dissipated pleasures of extravagance.

Scattered throughout this natural botanical garden are villas controlled by smart technology. Their interiors, walled with clear glass, are comfort-controlled with air conditioning, yet it feels as if the living space is al fresco. The central facilities are connected by well-groomed paths, traveled by electric service

vehicles. Each villa is equipped with high-tech terminals, creating a complex network like a nervous system. And there's no annoying password entry requirement each time you connect with the Internet. It's smoothly connected to everywhere on the planet. Technology doesn't compete with nature; instead, as we make progress, it will become more compatible with nature, and the boundary between them will blur. As the fusion deepens to the point that we don't know where nature ends and human agency begins, our sensibilities will be able to move freely between them. To that end, we must consider architecture that authentically accepts the gifts of nature. That challenge would surely interest architects. Agriculture is also practiced within the park. It would be ideal if local people were to work here. Restaurants and spas could be developed that use organically grown local vegetables, herbs, and medicinal plants. I'd like the spa to be based on Asian-style medical treatment.

This hotel is not just a place to relax; it's also a place for productive, concentrated work. That is, it's a resort that simultaneously allows both "on" and "off" modes. As far as I can see, Asia's energetic workers don't take long vacations like Westerners do; they certainly don't take days off. They find meaning in their work, drawing their ambition and vitality from it. They have projects going in various places, and live on the move: today Beijing, tomorrow Jakarta, two nights in Tokyo, and then back to Shanghai. It's not that they're busy. They are the "new nomads." They rest while they're working.

What if we think of work-related intellectual activity not as labor, but as a time of fulfillment? If we consider it refreshing to spend time reading or writing a manuscript without a deadline, this botanical resort seems an excellent place for such activities. Swimming in the pool, taking a walk or run in a stunning natural setting, dining – in all of these moments, leisure coexists with creation.

In fact, a project based on this idea is already underway on a certain island in Indonesia. The plan is to develop not a whole island, but a hillside facing the sea or a large swath of gently sloping land according to a completely novel concept. I was commissioned to work on vision building. What emerged was the large-scale botanical garden and high-tech villas described above. It might sound like a dream, and it will probably take a long time to realize it. But design is the articulation of a dream and the expression of the path to its realization.

Now, with Asia's era almost certainly arriving, I would like to focus on a new realm of pleasure, one making full use of our aesthetic resources in order to transcend the forms of desire bequeathed by colonialism. What kind of resort will we see then?

National Parks

How will we make the best use of the Japanese archipelago? This is an eternal challenge for Japan, whose location is distinctive from the perspective of global topography. There are four main islands: Kyushu, Shikoku, Honshu, and Hokkaido. Because of their relative proximity, they have been united in a chain by undersea tunnels and gigantic bridges. To understand the perspective of those living on them, it's important to recognize that originally, they were not thought of as islands, but as broader and more spacious lands – countries – isolated from the outer world by the sea. The term "island" (*shima* or *to*) is used to refer to the multitude of smaller islands surrounding these four main islands.

We have a clear concept of borders, since our national borders are defined by the sea; they separate us from Korea, China, and Russia. North America is also a distant neighbor. This is why we have such a strong sense of being clearly

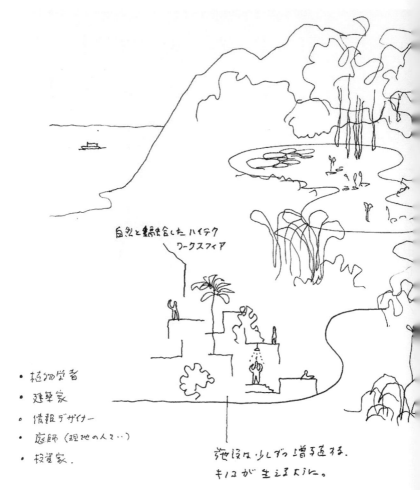

自然と融合したハイテク
ワークスフィア

- 植物学者
- 建築家
- 情報デザイナー
- 庭師（現地の人で…）
- 投資家.

施設は少しずつ増殖する.
キノコが生えるように.

〈 Botanical Worksphere 〉

植物園＋ホテル. ただし, リゾートホテルというよりも.
ここで仕事ができる. きわめてスムーズ, スマートなハイテク環境が整っている.
人は必ずしも, アトラクションや遊びのメニューを期待しない. 素晴しい環境で働きたい.

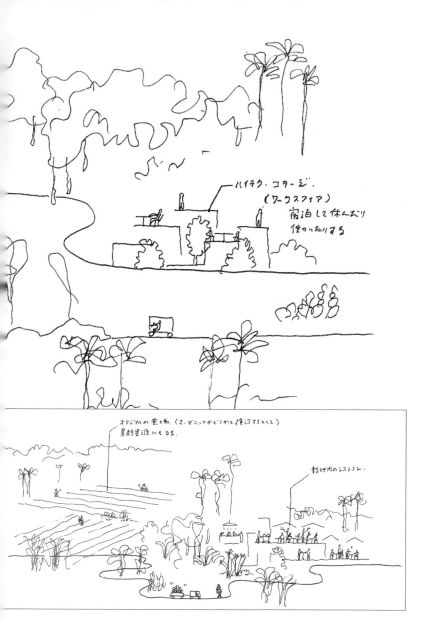

ハイテク、コラージ゛.
(ワークスフィア)
宿泊して休んだり
使ったりする

オリジナルの栗工場。(オーガニックかどうかは検討するとして)
景観資源にもなる.

敷地内のレストラン.

independent from the rest of the world. This naturally fostered an intense national identity, fortified even further by the Japanese language.

Our climate and natural features are also distinctive. Prevailing winds meet the rugged mountain ranges, producing rain and snow, which feed the thick forests covering much of the country. Rich in water, Japan is also extremely mountainous, and in comparison to larger and more powerful continental rivers, ours run like capillaries from the mountains to the sea, flowing rapidly and nimbly like waterfalls. This land, born of volcanic activity, is richly varied and hot springs gush forth everywhere.

Agriculture based on rice cultivation harnessing the moist climate has supported life in Japan for millennia. From the Jomon period through the Yayoi (c. 14,000 BCE–c. 300 CE), rice cultivation sustained Japanese lives until our transformation into an industrial nation. By carefully exploiting the richness of the four seasons by changing and modifying how we live in response, we have slowly nurtured a unique culture in harmony with its topography and climate. We have lived with our senses attuned to nature, in winter threshing straw, in spring enjoying the dawn, in summer sewing the lightweight cotton kimono known as *yukata*, and in autumn silently admiring the moon. In China, dynasties changed one after another, with the governing ethnic groups changing in turn; in contrast, Japan has preserved a single nation from ancient times to the present day.

After World War II, when Japan experienced its first defeat, the broad Pacific Coastal Zone, stretching from the southern Kanto plain along the coast of Honshu to the Tokai and Setouchi regions and northern Kyushu, was established as a stronghold of industrial production. In these areas, petrochemical complexes were built, businesses were invited to build factories and warehouses, and modern harbor facilities were constructed, so that natural resources could be imported and processed, and the resulting products could be efficiently exported. The four major industrial zones were Keihin (Tokyo–Yokohama), Chukyo (Nagoya and environs), Hanshin (Osaka–Kobe), and Kitakyushu (northern Kyushu). The Shinkansen high-speed rail lines and a system of expressways were established as major transportation arteries. As a result, Japan clearly achieved industrialized nation status, eventually ranking as the second-largest economic power in the world.

However, this growth came at a cost; Japan was tremendously polluted by effluents from waterfront factories and chemical substances emitted into the air. Concrete revetment walls in the port areas spread beyond where they were really necessary, transforming the seaside into a bleak, industrial landscape. The national budget has been spent in moving both things and people, securing energy supplies and reducing the risk of natural disaster. Consequently, in just the last sixty years, Japan has acquired the brutal guise of an artificial industrial archipelago.

Not only the sea and rivers were polluted. Just as the waterfronts were turned into concrete barriers, our everyday lives and cities were also defiled by roads and dams considered essential to the promotion of industry and national progress, as well as urbanization, which simply ignored any sense of harmony with the environment. The messy glut of commercial buildings and signage in public spaces approved to speed up economic growth numbed our connection with the landscape, and developed like a scab of insensitivity and dullness over the sensibilities of the Japanese people. This has given rise to the observation that contemporary Japanese are keenly attuned to small-scale beauty, but unfazed by large-scale ugliness.

In traditional culture, as well as in individual instances of design and architecture, Japan has exhibited an extremely high level of creativity and sophistication, but the resulting overall scenery, in which all of these should be combined, is ugly. This trend is not confined to cities. One might even say that rural areas, in the effort to imitate urban areas, simply expose a certain lack of refinement. Despite its rich nature, the Japanese countryside presents many bleak landscapes too.

To restore this land to a climate of peace and repose, we first have to do some cleaning. Japanese sensibilities are intrinsically delicate, thorough, precise, and simple. If we become more attuned to these traits, we can make the next step forward for our economy and culture.

There are twenty-nine national parks in Japan. The first time I became aware of them, I was a boy, collecting stamps. The stamps were modest and monochrome, but in a corner of my memory, a series featuring the parks' beautiful scenery in condensed form still remains. Because intrinsically, every mountain and every inlet is beautiful, people may wonder why we deliberately designate a specific area as a national park. The Minister of the Environment defines national parks as "the places of greatest natural scenic beauty, including areas in the sea, representing the model scenic beauty of our country." I am somewhat embarrassed at the nation defining nature in terms of "model scenic beauty," but these landscapes do evoke deep emotion in me.

The United States is the birthplace of national parks. Between the mid-nineteenth century and the early twentieth century, laws were passed to protect the scenery, nature, animals, and so forth in Yellowstone and the Grand Canyon. A century after U.S. independence, the people who had hacked open the frontier, keen to record their history, woke up to the natural wonder of the North American continent and resolved to protect it.

I'm not sure if it is through the influence of this idea or not, but the information design relating to the national parks in the United States is orderly and beautiful, clearly distinguishing the parks from both commercialism and nostalgia. Underlying it is the visionary work of the great graphic designer Massimo Vignelli. He developed the basis for the National Parks publication design. Specifically, he strove to enhance the readability and aesthetic quality of maps and to organize the layout of type and photographs to arrive at a rational, coherent system for production of pamphlets and other media.

The goal of information design is to empower the user. Certain information is sought by anyone visiting national parks. Vignelli created an aesthetically pleasing, practical system that provides ten basic brochure formats accommodating this information. It's more significant that the communication design system he created was not under the sole control of one designer, but available for voluntary study and use by the staff who manage and operate individual parks. Following this illustrious precedent, there have been further improvements and successes in the information design of U.S. national parks.

When people have a readable and attractive information tool in hand when they head for a national park, they are able to connect with the consciousness of many other people through that experience. I dare say that the national parks are not nature itself; we might see them as an intangible chain reaction of awareness formed within human consciousness regarding how to interact with and savor nature. In this sense, national parks can also be considered an aggregate of high-level design.

Design is often talked about in the context of competition to enhance the appeal of products, but in fact, it has a strong ethical dimension in terms of our shared social values. Values like restraint, dignity, and pride are quite close to the essence of design. National parks should not engage in a public relations competition through excessive visuals or poorly designed logos, but instead should quietly and precisely facilitate connection. When information design truly functions, it becomes invisible. Otherwise, the information turns into noise, degrading the quality of communication.

In 1985, Massimo Vignelli received the first Presidential Design Award for his work for the national parks. A quarter century beforehand, the United States had begun to develop information design for the national parks. In Japan, I'm sure there are various issues, but I think it's about time we rekindle awareness of our national parks. It's a perfect theme for reconsidering our land and country with aesthetic sense as a starting point.

Having experienced its era of industrial prosperity, Japan must formulate a new vision of itself as a more aesthetically sophisticated country, a country of hospitality. A solid first step in this direction will be to create national parks as information architecture, rather than areas defined by staking them out as physical locations. That this task is incomplete is a blessing. Fortunately, the possibilities for media have greatly expanded. And in this, we are beginning to see enormous potential.

The Setouchi Triennale

Beginning on July 19, 2010, the Setouchi Triennale, a contemporary art festival, was held for 105 consecutive days on seven islands in the Seto Inland Sea (Seto Naikai), as well as in the city of Takamatsu on Shikoku, one of Japan's four main islands. It bustled with attendees in almost unimaginable numbers. It's difficult to decide how one should measure the success of an event, but this one drew more than three times the number of visitors expected: 938,000 instead of 300,000. At least in terms of ticket sales, it was a huge success.

The seven islands of Naoshima, Teshima, Inujima, Megijima, Ogijima, Shodoshima, and Oshima are located in the Seto Inland Sea between Okayama prefecture (on the main island of Honshu) and Kagawa prefecture, on Shikoku. Born in the city of Okayama (the prefectural capital), I used to go camping on the islands with my friends in the summer, so I was excited when I heard about the festival. Then Fram Kitagawa, general director of the Triennale, commissioned me for the communication tools, including posters and logos; my interest turned into actual work.

That said, the centerpiece of this international festival is contemporary art and those who organize, support, and participate in it. My state of mind would be similar to that of a welcoming host; I was naturally motivated to do this unobtrusive background work. Furthermore, because the Seto Inland Sea is Japan's oldest and largest officially designated national park, I was motivated to design the Triennale as very precise information architecture. It would be an information platform facilitating carefree travel around the islands for maximum enjoyment of the festival.

My first goal was to create serene key visuals. I invited photographer Yoshihiko Ueda to shoot them. After scouting some locations, Ueda and I chartered a Cessna and flew over the islands. The landscape is familiar, usually photographed from a small set of well-established locations, so it's very difficult to take fresh pictures of the Inland Sea. We conceived a tilted bird's-eye view that could capture the islands dotting the sea in a new way. Just as we thought, viewed from a small plane, they were sublimely beautiful, as if seen from the ancient world of Japan's creation myth.

On the day of our flight, it was calm, and the border between sea and sky dissolved, creating a harmonious gradation. In that vast space, the islands were lush with deep greenery. We felt ourselves completely engulfed. Approaching Megijima, we happened to see two passenger ferries sailing in parallel. They left two white wakes. Hearing the shutter clicks from the back seat, I knew Ueda had gotten the shot. From these photos, people will intuitively understand the significance of this festival.

The essence of this event is in the experience of cruising the islands by ferry. This is the overarching plan for the Setouchi Triennale. The islands are close together in the calm waters of the Inland Sea. It seems that many people, particularly Westerners, associate the word archipelago with the Aegean Sea. Indeed, the Aegean islands, with their unique scenery and light, are beautiful, but there is also a great distance between them. The real pleasure of the Setouchi art cruise is that because the islands are only fifteen or twenty minutes apart by ferry, you can visit them easily and experience simultaneously the art and the charm of the islands. The scenic beauty of one of Japan's first national parks is enough to give visitors a special impression. Key visuals must convey this at a glance.

However, there was an important issue that had to be cleared up if the festival was not to become a crucible of confusion. Depopulation has been a real cause of concern for these rural communities, so it's impossible for tens of thousands of visitors to pour into the area and expect to move about freely. It's not as if you are just going to one island and then turning around and going home. Attendees have to become light-hearted "island hop-pers," jumping from island to island. The freedom of movement we experience on land, via taxi, bike, or on foot, is curtailed on the water. In the Inland Sea, there are plenty of companies oper-ating ferry services, but their proprietary route systems are sur-prisingly complex and inflexible.

In short, this is a *marine transportation event*. That's why I gave higher priority to information design centered on transportation than I did to the main visuals. The logo was always accompanied by a dynamic subvisual indicating the trans-portation routes tying the islands together. I also tried to make the information tools for transportation as user-friendly as pos-sible. On the logistics side, the city of Takamatsu took the initia-tive in negotiating with the ferry companies to increase the number of ferry trips on many routes. On the design side, I arranged the routes and timetables into an easily understandable diagram. I then developed a free-download app for mobile phones and touchscreen devices.

Of further importance was the map. People arriving at the individual islands' ports can use buses and other public trans-portation, but for the most part have to set out on foot to visit and enjoy the various art sites. Such explorations are the reality of the Setouchi Triennale. That's why we had to offer maps that were far more detailed than Google Earth, easy to understand, and beautiful.

In the set of maps we created, the one with the highest resolution shows individual houses; from there the scale goes up to the village level, then the individual islands, and finally the overall tour routes for visiting all seven islands – each map clearly designed for specific use. On electronic devices, visitors could go from the dwelling level to the island level by pinching in and out. But although portable terminals and electronic devices are handy, not everyone has one, and many are unfamiliar with their operation. So the same resolution images were printed as a folding map that fit inside a pass case to be worn on a lanyard around the neck. We carefully selected the materials for the case, the lanyard, and even the hook fittings. A folding map in a pass case is pretty easy and fun to use, and assuming that the wireless signal would be weak in some areas, it would be an essential information tool.

The success of this design could be measured by the number of attendees exploring the islands with this indispensable item suspended from their necks. The set of maps achieved the goal of empowering the user, serving as a guide to the festival and to the works of art that were the focus of the Setouchi Triennale. I heard that right before the event closed, when it was extremely crowded, some ferries were not able to accommodate all the visitors and there was some confusion involving ticket sales. Three times more people showed up than were expected – the type of situation for which a contingency plan will be developed in the future.

The first Setouchi Triennale was a success, but the plan to develop the Seto islands as a contemporary art zone originated long ago, in 1985. Its origin was a concept to develop Naoshima through an agreement between Chikatsugu Miyake, then mayor of Naoshima, and Tatsuhiko Fukutake, the founder of Fukutake Shoten (now Benesse Holdings). At the time, unease was spreading among the island's citizens because of the establishment of an industrial waste disposal site, as well as environmental pollution from the sulfur dioxide emitted by a metal-smelting operation in the northern part of the island. It had been reported that neighboring Teshima was facing grave environmental pollution caused by the illegal dumping of industrial waste. Under these circumstances, Fukutake's idea of making the Seto islands a gathering place for children and Miyake's idea to develop the southern part of Naoshima into a clean and educational cultural area overlapped.

The concept of making the Seto islands a children's place first took shape as an overnight nature experience zone, Naoshima International Campground. There the plan began to move forward with the construction of a Mongolian dwelling called a *pao*, under the supervision of the architect Tadao Ando.

With Soichiro Fukutake, currently the spokesman for Benesse Art Site, inheriting his father's vision, the cultural village moved forward as a place where contemporary art can flourish. With the completion of Benesse House (1992), which combined hotel guest rooms with a space for exhibiting contemporary art, and the Benesse House Oval (1995), a lodge, the stunning news that a genuine base for modern art had been created on this small island in the Seto Inland Sea was broadcast to the world, and Naoshima began to garner interest as an important part of

Japan's distinctive contemporary art scene. Then, with the completion of the Chichu Art Museum (2004), Naoshima enhanced its presence as a cultural site attracting global attention. All of the architecture for these facilities was designed by Tadao Ando. The distinguishing feature is that most of the buildings, set partially underground, blend into the natural surroundings. In addition, with the *Ie* (House) Project, in which existing traditional homes are repurposed as art sites, contemporary art in Naoshima has left the museum and entered daily life on the island, where it has begun to permeate the consciousness of the people.

Once new art museums were created on neighboring Inujima and Teshima with the vision of an even more comprehensive Setouchi Art Network, the possibility of a greater art zone uniting the region was revealed. In 2008, on Inujima, a museum designed by the architect Hiroshi Sambuichi preserved and breathed new life into the ruins of an abandoned copper smelter. And in 2010, on Teshima, an innovative museum honoring the special characteristics of the land was created through a collaboration between the artist Rei Naito and Tokyo-based architect Ryue Nishizawa. A museum devoted to the work of the artist Lee Ufan, designed by Tadao Ando, also opened that year.

Thanks to astounding powers of conception and realization, the Seto Inland Sea has rapidly matured as an art zone. The islands and the sea are already beginning to connect institutions like the Ohara Museum of Art in Okayama, the Isamu Noguchi Garden Museum of Art in Takamatsu, and Marugame's Genichiro Inokuma Contemporary Art Museum. Apparently, plans have already been made for subsequent iterations of the Setouchi Triennale, designed to be held every three years, up through the fifth. I think that these events represent a fantastic example of how to make the most of the Japanese islands. Based on my experience with this project, I feel that my imagination will really take off in the creation of information design for the national parks.

Map of Megijima from the navigation tool for the Setouchi Triennale

Chapter 5

Future Materials: Designing Experience

Media Trigger Creativity

Human creativity is triggered by the materials at hand. Take stone in the Stone Age, for instance. We tend to imagine that stone was used from the very beginning of the Stone Age. But for humans who had just begun to walk upright, stone must have been a decisive medium that awakened them to the use of their hands. For human hands recently freed by the fact of upright posture, stone's durability, weight, and suitability for processing made it the ideal material for inviting imagination or creativity. I presume that stone's hardness and weight led to the desire to destroy or cut objects, and its texture and tactile qualities awakened our sensibilities to the satisfaction of using tools. Ultimately, *stone* stimulated our hands and minds and became the driving force of the Stone Age.

The act of making stone tools did not end with simply making; it must have triggered the mindfulness to improve that making, functionally and aesthetically. A stone knife was made by using one stone to chip or polish another, but the level of balance and perfection attained gives satisfaction even today, tens of thousands of years later. These are the deep emotions I feel regarding a variety of excavated stone tools.

The same is true of paper. Today, magazines, newspapers, and books are called print media, but I feel uncomfortable with that term because it burdens paper with associations to the outmoded aspects of old media. Paper certainly triggered human creativity through its relation with the written word, but its appeal is not to be summed up by the fact that it can supply pages to be printed. Paper's original power of inspiration lies in its whiteness and its resilience. There are few white objects in nature, so paper stands out for its extraordinary whiteness. To produce this blinding white, people in Asia learned to beat and unravel the bark fibers, soak them in water, scoop them out with a bamboo-framed screen, and dry them in the sun. Paper's resilience is such that it stands taut when grasped between the fingers. Yet this whiteness and resilience is also easily soiled and torn; its existence is extremely fragile.

On this thin and graceful white tautness, people draw pictures or write characters or letters with jet-black ink. This is a leap toward irreversibility, to a place from which there is no turning back – a series of tactile responses that continuously make one aware of the moment when something implicit becomes explicit and comes to fruition. Paper always gives people a tension akin to that felt in a packed concert hall that's fallen silent just before a solo violinist plays the first note. Failure is always possible, but a splendid performance will soar all the more brilliantly on white paper.

Paper's inspirational power fostered in the human sensibility the capacity to write words, draw pictures, and set type. Paper has taught us preparedness, determination, deportment, and sensitivity to both eternity and the present moment. The lessons continue today.

I call media like this – materials that evoke our creative urges – "senseware." When I think of various senseware, including bronze, porcelain, and iron, my heart soars, but here I'd like to discuss a new senseware, synthetic fibers, and the industrial possibilities they offer.

The textile industry has been one of Japan's key industries, but that situation is changing considerably. When Japan's labor force was much cheaper than that of Europe or the United States, its textiles were like China's products today. As captured in *Joko Aishi* (The Tragic History of the Mill Girls), a report published in 1925, at one time young women, working long hours at low wages, supported Japan's production of cheap textiles. After World War II, synthetic textile production brought great prosperity. However, the era of ¥360 to the U.S. dollar is long past; in 2011, Japan's enormous economic power propelled the yen to a peak rate of less than ¥80 to the dollar. While this means we are able to purchase goods from around the world and travel the globe with ease, in terms of producing goods and selling them to the world, everyone recognizes we are in a tough situation.

At some point, Japan's textile industry lost its lead to Taiwan and Korea, and in recent years, they in turn have ceded that position to China and India, countries with even lower labor costs. With capital investment, standard textile production can be carried out in any country, so most of the familiar textiles used in our clothing today are not made in Japan. But Japan's textile industry is not in decline. In fact, in the effort to improve production technology, it is seeking to open up new markets, exploring the most innovative new synthetic fibers.

Fibers can be broadly divided into two types: natural and synthetic. For the former, the origin of the raw material is natural: silk, cotton, hemp, and wool. For synthetic fibers, the raw material is usually petroleum, and their names, like nylon and polyester, carry a chemical image. In recent years, there has been great evolution in synthetic fibers to the point that it's hard to tell the difference from natural fibers just by touch.

In the past, synthetic fibers were generally positioned as substitutes for materials like silk that were expensive to produce. When silk stockings were replaced by nylons, their affordability and durability were welcomed, and synthetic fibers expanded into many areas of daily life. On the other hand, it's not easy to surpass the gifts of nature. Praise for the texture of natural fibers like cotton and hemp plays like a figured bass, holding one corner of public opinion, and many who hold this view hate even to utter the word polyester. However, synthetic fibers are more than a substitute for natural fibers. Maturing technology will reconcile the opposition between the artificial and the natural, and will move toward erasing the boundary between them. As technology continues to evolve, products with unique features that can't be evaluated on the same plane as natural fibers are being developed.

Japan's textile businesses have begun to operate in a broader field of activity, beyond clothing; they're producing even more original high-performance textiles used as materials in a wide range of technologies. A few examples are carbon fiber for airplane fuselages; aramid fibers for wind turbine propellers, bullet-proof vests, and firefighters' uniforms; microfibers for cleaning oil films; hollow fiber membranes for high-precision filtration; elastic fibers that harden like an injection-molded sponge and produce a soft cushion; optical fibers that don't attenuate light as it passes through; and electrically conductive fibers. By continually developing fibers that can anticipate the future, textile businesses are successively opening doors to new territories.

Most people don't understand the highly technical roles played by these high-performance fibers; used in applications like turbine propellers and airplane fuselages, and as artificial blood vessels in advanced medicine, these fibers seldom affect the life of the average person. So even though Japan's textile industry has been successful in developing advanced-function fibers using sophisticated technology, the majority of these fibers are unsung heroes supporting today's lifestyles and environment.

I was asked for advice on gaining a bit more visibility for these fibers. At the beginning of 2006, the Ministry of Economy, Trade and Industry (METI) approached me to see if I might stage a public appeal to the potential inherent in Japan's synthetic fibers, if possible at a venue where it could attract consumer attention like the fashion industry does.

In order to spotlight the textile industry's growth potential, Japan's cutting-edge textiles should keep their distance from the fashion industry as it's conceived in France and Italy, and instead highlight the unique realm of creativity these new industrial materials have opened up, bringing awareness to the appeal and added value of synthetic fibers.

To achieve this, it's important to show synthetic fibers in a format in which their properties can be easily seen and understood, not as an imitation of natural fibers but as a completely new thing – senseware. And it's important to use unique methods to demonstrate how senseware can stimulate people's creativity. In this era of the strong yen, I thought we should craft a storyline to help people understand the singular properties of these materials by mobilizing Japan's outstanding manufacturing talent and technology.

I always argue that I design experiences, not things. That's why this work is so fitting. Design is the craft of evaluating the essence of things, and when it is commissioned to focus on the vision of industry, it has to visualize the dormant potential of that industry. This is how plans for the exhibition of synthetic fibers began to take shape.

Fashion and Fibers

What is fashion, anyway? This thought suddenly came to mind when I was asked to put high-tech materials at the leading edge of fashion. Is it something to do with lifestyles, or with the workings of the industry? Or is it an issue of fads or trends?

When I was young, I subscribed to the French edition of *Vogue*. It was my way of trying to figure out what fashion is. Of course, there's a limit to the knowledge you can gain from a magazine, but I could sense a rational principle behind the editing of *Vogue*. There is a tacit premise that fashion isn't clothing or accessories but rather the competition and rapport among human sensibilities. Sometimes I came across photos that deeply impressed me with the sense that this was indeed actually the art of life. Of course, *Vogue* also included articles about trends, but the ones that especially attracted my attention were reports about events in the world of high society – articles dealing not with models, but documentaries of fashion involving real people immersed in society. Among those society figures, the most strikingly idiosyncratic and impressive to me were never the young and svelte. In those who had already settled into old age, I sensed a magnificence and vigor like that emanating from grand old trees.

Human beings are born with certain inclinations, and live with biases and peculiarities, but those who take all this in stride and push on through acquire a powerful presence. They have an intensely human aura that far surpasses physical charms enhanced by cosmetic surgery. Such people can carry the power of haute couture into which talented designers have poured their heart and soul. They meet head-on the challenge of designers of radical and creative clothing who seem to say, "If you can rock it, go for it!" amplifying those efforts with their own personal style and releasing that energy into their surroundings.

The models are chosen not simply for their figures or their charm; they have been selected because they possess an almost irritatingly powerful presence. It is as if their eyes have toyed with each and every human sin, all of which burden them; their lips appear to have released thousands of idiocies and yet sometimes let slip electrifying profundities. Their limbs are so long as to seem unbalanced, and they seem altogether far from loveliness, purity, and innocence. And yet they overflow with an irresistible charm. Gifted photographers quietly and precisely harvest their allure, sparing nothing. I get goosebumps from such photos and am unable to look away.

The more I look at such magazines, the more I think fashion is the art of life, and that rather than being stylish, I would like to become a person with presence. It's an extreme metaphor, but gaining belly fat as you age is natural. The sense of security and humor of a potbelly is unavailable to thin, young men, so if an older man is able to confidently present himself, he can be sexy and fashionable. I've always thought this way. So I was bemused when formally commissioned to manage an exhibition focusing on fashion developments. To look at fashion as an industry, we need to reconsider it from scratch.

Essentially, fashion is the art of life, but it's also an industry that's created huge economic benefits. Threads are spun from natural fibers, woven into cloth in a multitude of ways, and then, at the hand of gifted designers, presented as clothing in a myriad of styles, which are eventually disseminated to the world on the waves of trends. As raw material is transformed into fashionable clothing, a dazzling number of added values are generated, creating a huge economy.

With the maturity of modern society, fashion trends have materialized over the past two or three hundred years, but the history of the fashion industry is not that long. Modern fashion, centered in France, commenced with the opening of Coco Chanel's boutique only a little over century ago. However, the Chanel era, when couture and its concept became an image shock wave that swept the globe with tsunamis of genuine fads, was short-lived; gradually fashion has turned into something more calculated, which is why branding has become an industry.

To directly experience the workings of the fashion industry, I briefly visited Première Vision, a major fabric trade show held in Paris. Textiles are classified into genres like tailored, elastic, and denim, as well as unique categories including "just made it into the show," and displayed as entirely practical materials. There was no clothing displayed, perhaps because that would be just noise, but attendees were allowed to take fabric swatches labeled with detailed information. Attendees are designers from the fashion houses, their top assistants, and fabric buyers. I wondered if they were coming up with new ideas for clothing as they looked over the materials, or searching for the perfect fabric to match images they already had in mind.

Six to seven hundred companies form the exhibitor base at this gigantic trade show. The textiles featured at Première Vision have been made in accordance with a previously planned "fashion scenario" announced at the show, along with a selection of trending colors. All of this is put together in an expensive information package, which is available for sale.

Fashion issuing from Paris is planned and produced by a Trend Setting Commission. The trends are drafted by "trend writers" with the sensibility and expertise to stay keenly aware of creative trends around the world, but the commission also includes textile industry leaders and government officials. Its operations reflect industry trends and the leading sensibilities of the times. My acquaintance Li Edelkoort, who chairs a company called Trend Union, is a well-known trend writer, and I am always impressed by her stories and commentary on trends.

As long as the raw material of fashion trends strikes a chord in people's minds, it doesn't matter what it is, whether it be the beautiful hues of bird feathers, or Buddhist images, or the combination of medical bandages with veins showing through pale skin. One video presented "senior" fashions. Mick Jagger of the Rolling Stones is in his early seventies, but he doesn't seem a bit like an ordinary senior. In fact, he has the kind of charisma a young person could never pull off. The crow's feet, his weathered body, the sensitivity and intelligence built up over years of living – trend writers carefully search out these sorts of things, write them up, and select color schemes. Jagger's video might make some people think, "I can't wait till I get old!"

Each creation is first developed at the raw material level, and every step must reflect the new fashion scenario – the story – beginning with the process that is the farthest upstream: thread production. Then fabric is woven from thread dyed in a trending color. It must be decided what hue, texture, and textiles are the most fitting to boost the story. If at this point all the paths are not aligned, cloth of an inharmonious color will circulate, a mood-breaking texture will attract attention, and the trending wave will come to nothing. The potential for added value is only as high as this wave.

The scenario is woven into the textiles, and the clothing is designed to cleave to this same scenario. The couture houses of Paris and Milan assemble talented designers and apprentices from around the world, and whether they follow or resist it, there is a single information axis, transmitted globally from the information launch pads known as the Paris Collection and the Milano Collection, around which clothing creation revolves.

The creativity of the clothing is multiplied by the creativity of criticism; glowing words will help formidable pieces of work get noticed and vault ahead. Fashion vocabulary is integrated into the journalism of Paris and Milan.

A multitude of Japanese fashion journalists go to places like this to collect information. This is how "upstream" and "downstream" are created in the flow of fashion information. For even outstanding fashion designers, being based in Japan means their work will remain unknown to the rest of the world; powerful designers have traveled to Paris or Milan to have their work announced. The Japanese mass media calls this being "valued by the world."

In recent years, media diversification and changes in consumer culture have ignited changes in the flow of information. Frequently, minor trends with major impact originate in Harajuku backstreet fashion, or we witness a phenomenon like the Tokyo Girls Collection, in which fashion evolves from the fresh interaction between the transmitters and recipients of information.

As for Japan's advanced fibers, we can't expect them to be "valued by the world." Following the established fashion information flow simply accelerates the industrial prosperity of France and Italy, so we should pursue *functioning in the world* rather than being valued by the world. First off, Japan must take the initiative to create an information flow about these unique new fibers. And it's essential to keep "fashion" at arm's length, giving birth to a new field of creation not limited to clothing but embracing human beings in a broader sense, through their living space. We have to discover new value and excitement at the intersection of people, the environment, and fiber.

Better to Be a Chicken's Beak

Lately I've been conscious of the need to take the initiative to function in the world rather than being valued by the world. In the passivity of being valued or evaluated, there is a sense of *amae*, a Japanese word indicating the reassuring dependence on something like a great power or culture. The saying, "It's better to be a chicken's beak than a cow's rump" appears in the Chinese classic the *Shiji* (*Records of the Grand Historian*), and it means it's better to be the head of a small organization than the tail of a large one. In any realm, be it finance, energy, fashion, or design, when we stand before the bedrock of the accumulated wisdom and power of Western culture, we tend to become timid. And the more we learn and assimilate, the more we tend to become the cow's rump. Of course, it's important to study with humility. But there are situations in which it's better to behave like the chicken, which, though small, thrusts its beak forward with determination.

The accumulation of Western culture is certainly overwhelming at times, and its mechanisms for the worldwide diffusion of industry and culture are remarkable. But the world needs more than this. Even a modest culture that developed at the eastern edge of Asia can contribute to the rest of the world, and if so, we should make it function in the places where it's needed. The world always needs new ideas. There are ways in which the modes of thought of Western civilization have led the world to an impasse. We should refrain from extravagance and hubris, but sometimes it's also necessary to spank a stagnant world to open its eyes to a different sense of values. This is what I mean by functioning rather than being valued.

I began as a graphic designer, but I've worked in the communications field for a long time, involved in the creation of experiences rather than objects. My work serves to imprint values and impressions in people's minds via events, exhibitions, and brand building.

The word "image" may sound trivial, but the world is made up of images, not objects. Hermès, Apple, India's Tata Motors, Bordeaux wine, five-star hotels, and sumo tournaments: what is in people's minds is an architecture of images, and a strong, well-made image is built up carefully and with great attention to detail.

The principle that drives an image is neither alchemy nor ingenious brand management but an active and passionate persistence in doing things, whether the passion comes from a group or an individual. Experience design, my work, turns a persistent will, like an undying flame, into a vivid image, allowing it to permeate the depths of people's minds and emotions. Each creative act – whether of logos, books, package design, or exhibitions – is only a part of that work.

As I undertook these activities, I began to sense the possibility of another large-scale creation, one that would gather diverse talents and technologies from around the world for a specific goal, editing the whole gamut of contributions into a series of related information bundles, and releasing it into the world as a grand living message.

The 2000 exhibition *RE DESIGN: Daily Products of the 21st Century* served as a catalyst for me to launch other exhibition projects. It was an invitation to awaken consciousness of the density of wisdom accumulated in everyday life, through an exhibition of experimental redesigns of objects of daily use. About twenty creators participated; by interweaving this diversity of thought and sensibility, I felt I'd struck a vein. The message surpassed my expectations by permeating into all corners of the world.

This was followed by other exhibitions, including *HAPTIC: Awakening the Senses*, *FILING: Chaos Management*, *JAPAN CAR: Designs for the Crowded Globe*, and so forth. *TOKYO FIBER / SENSEWARE* is an extension of this series. Each time I dispatched one of these messages, I felt aware of Japan at its core, or perhaps, Asia. I've used the words "delicacy," "thoroughness," "precision," and "simplicity" to describe Japan's sensibility, but it is Asia that stresses not just efficiency but also atmosphere and feeling, and in Asia there is a sensibility that apprehends the world openly and generously, perceiving that the natural and the artificial are not in opposition.

In response to an appeal from the Ministry of Economy, Trade and Industry (METI), I produced the exhibition *TOKYO FIBER / SENSEWARE* twice, in 2007 and in 2009. The first time it was held in Tokyo and Paris; the second in Tokyo and Milan, and it went to Holon, Israel, as a traveling exhibition. In all cases, I conceived of a new creation unrestricted by conventional categories like fashion, interiors, and products, but broadly rebundling people, textiles, and the environment. I planned to present a concrete future via the form of exhibits not readily classifiable as furniture, clothing, or products.

Participants represented a truly diverse range of fields; among them were not only individual creators, including architects, designers, and media artists, but also manufacturers of high-tech consumer electronics, auto manufacturers, virtual reality researchers, botanical artists, dancers, and so on. Although it's not easy to get exceptionally talented individuals and companies with proven track records to participate, it was my role to carefully craft the project's appeal and goals to stimulate interest and initiative commensurate with the extent of their participation. I wanted to stage an exhibition of the results of creativity brought forth by interweaving multiple talents and professions, technologies and sensibilities, and send it out into the world as if launching a satellite.

We produced another *TOKYO FIBER* exhibition, in 2009.

In this version, all seven major members of the Japan Chemical Fibers Association participated: Teijin, Toray, Asahi Kasei, Mitsubishi Rayon, Unitika, Toyobo, and Kuraray all played major roles in the exhibition and provided materials.

The 2007 exhibition had managed to showcase a range of enchanting and lyrical fibers. However, several major manufacturers said that if we really wanted to give expression to Japanese textiles we should present them as cutting-edge technologies, into which we could easily delve further. This led to a new exhibition featuring a lineup of advanced fibers. The project began with a material orientation from each participating manufacturer. The more I listened to their explanations of the advanced fibers that they were so eager to show the world, the more inspired I became.

Take the example of Asahi Kasei's non-woven cloth, SMASH; its high-thermal plasticity allows for amazingly dynamic three-dimensional molding. Techniques like embossing, which sculpts minute undulations in paper, are generally known as types of 3D modeling, but SMASH can be raised from its plane state to a height of about 4.6 centimeters. The flexibility of this fiber is astonishingly like that of plastic.

Toyobo's spring structure, BREATHAIR, is a three-dimensional block-like material produced by injection molding a high-elasticity monofilament fiber into bristle-shaped threads from a nozzle with a diameter of less than 1.3 millimeters. As soon as it leaves the nozzle, it solidifies into a fluffy substance that is 95 percent air. BREATHAIR seems like it could be a substitute for urethane or sponge. Injection molding is interesting. Currently, the material is being used for Shinkansen bullet train seat cushions.

The optical fiber ESKA, developed by Mitsubishi Rayon, has been used to create an exciting new building material. Austria-based building-material maker Luccon has developed technology for evenly layering large quantities of these optical fibers in concrete. The resulting product is a translucent concrete that is even stronger than its conventional counterpart. Given that concrete is known for blocking light and sound, the emergence of this material seems likely to completely transform architecture.

Teijin's NANOFRONT ultra-fine polyester nanofiber has an astounding feature: the diameter of a single fiber is 1/7,500 that of a human hair. Because cloth made of these nanofibers, which are invisible to the naked eye, has a surface area and void structure dozens of times greater than those of normal cloth, it easily absorbs oil film or fine dust less than one micron in diameter, exhibiting superb wiping performance.

Unitika's TERRAMAC is macromolecular material made from corn and other natural materials. It can be used like solid plastics for sheet-like molding, but when extruded from a nozzle as a fine filament woven with a special knitting technique, it can be used as a three-dimensional fabric. Because it is made from plant materials, it is readily biodegradable.

Kuraray's KURALON EC is an electro-conductive fiber. Incorporating metal nanoparticles, it retains strong conductivity and is resistant to bending and abrasion. Thanks to these kinds of materials, electric appliances can be more pliable. This fiber brings to mind images of new products coming to market, like a T-shirt with the word ON printed on the front, which, when pressed, flips a switch or jeans equipped with a soft fabric keyboard on the thigh.

Toray's carbon fiber TORAYCA is stronger and lighter than iron. It's used for a variety of purposes, from fishing rods to satellites. This material has a strength many times greater than metal at less than half the weight.

It's not one of the seven major companies, but Sakase Adtech has also developed an amazing product: triaxial woven fabric. Normally, fibers are positioned as warp and weft, then woven to create textiles, but triaxial fabric, woven with three sets of fibers at 120-degree angles, is like a crystallization of pure mathematics. When extremely pliable fibers are woven in this manner and press molded, the product is an extraordinarily beautiful 3D textile with a smooth tertiary surface. It's used for aerospace applications, as in satellites.

Clearly no ordinary textiles, these inspire imagination. An important job for design is to visualize latent possibilities, not to think about form after the purpose has been decided. Presented with such opportunities, I bubble over with enthusiasm.

Arriving at Japan's Future Overseas

TOKYO FIBER '09 / SENSEWARE, the show that visualized the merits of Japan's high-tech fibers, opened at the Milano Triennale.

We had expected to open it in Tokyo, but due to circumstances at that venue, the international opening came first. We chose the Triennale because the attention of the world's manufacturing industries is focused there. So that I would have no regrets, I wanted to deliver my message on a stage from which there was no escape.

The work of the participating creators was as rich as anticipated. Creating an exhibition concept, allocating the materials, and commissioning the manufacturing are like writing a script, deciding on the cast, and hiring the actors. The actors, in their own unique ways, assumed their roles, and with a performance that far exceeded expectations, incited the audience to erupt in applause.

Given SMASH, the non-woven textile made of extremely pliable, long polyester fibers, the fashion duo of mintdesigns created a 3D surgical mask. In recent years, more and more people have been wearing masks due to the proliferation of hay fever and the spread of influenza. The duo, which approaches clothing as product design, expressed this molding fiber's special characteristic – that it can be freely modeled into a three-dimensional shape – in an everyday product.

In the end, they made two masks, one modeled on a human face and the other on a monkey's. Both completely cover the bottom half of the face, including the nose. Wearing the human mask, anyone's features appear generally well ordered. When it's on, the wearer seems peculiarly composed. With the monkey mask, because the entire palate protrudes, there's

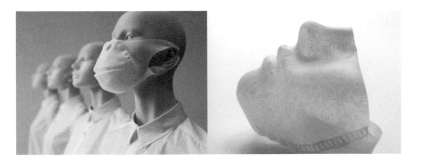

To Be Someone by mintdesigns; material: SMASH

generous space in the area covering the nose and the mouth so it's comfortable to wear. Anyone wearing this mask looks like a character from *Planet of the Apes*, giving fresh humor to the act of wearing a mask. The masks can also be printed with patterns for an even stronger statement. If you were to board a train calmly wearing a monkey mask with a colorful pattern, the other passengers wouldn't be able to look away. These masks were presented in their own collection.

The artist Yasuhiro Suzuki created *Fiber Being*, a "breathing" mannequin, using airy 3D BREATHAIR. Mannequins these days are so realistic that they enchant me, but unfortunately, they don't move. Suzuki's mannequins move. He made life-sized hollow dolls modeled on his own body, with spines of transparent acrylic, allowing them to stand on their own. The hollow interiors are filled with barely visible transparent threads interwoven with the 3D material like the fibers of a luffa, like a central nervous system, and controlled by computer. When the BREATHAIR

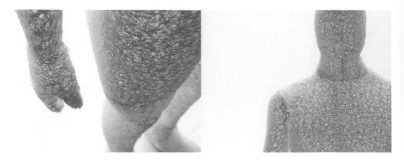

Yasuhiro Suzuki's *Fiber Being*; material: BREATHAIR

material is pulled at suitable intervals from below the floor, the bodies expand and contract, as if they were breathing. The audience simply stared, dumbfounded, as the three mysterious mannequins "breathed."

Makoto Azuma, a botanical artist whose work depends on fastidiously capturing the beauty of plants as contemporary art, created *Time of Moss*, a curvilinear moss wetland installation running through the center of the exhibition venue. He used the thick 3D woven carpet-like biodegradable TERRAMAC as artificial soil. To accomplish this, we had the floor of the venue raised fifteen centimeters. Because a marsh suddenly appears in that flat space covered with white carpet, you can't tell where the artificial ends and the natural begins.

Shigeru Ban took up the challenge of the carbon fiber TENAX. Known for his remarkable use of materials, Ban has repeatedly used recyclable cardboard tubes, and he designed the Centre Pompidou-Metz with an innovative wooden structure.

Makoto Azuma's installation *Time of Moss*; material: TERRAMAC

Carbon fiber has the highest tensile strength, but it's relatively expensive and difficult to use alone. So Ban attached carbon fiber 0.2 millimeters thick to the front and back of an aluminum panel 1.5 millimeters thick, producing an ultralight chair that a child could lift with his pinky. A sturdily built person like Ban can sit on the chair and it doesn't give an inch, but from the side, it looks as thin as wire.

Shigeru Ban's carbon-fiber chair; material: TENAX

Panasonic Corporation's Fukitorimushi, a robotic dust cloth; material: NANOFRONT

The architect Jun Aoki approached carbon fiber in a similarly innovative manner to that employed in his buildings, such as the façade of the Louis Vuitton flagship store in Tokyo, which introduced a unique elegance to the neighborhood. The result at the exhibition was a cantilevered lighting apparatus with a long straight arm, like that of a railway crossing gate. Aoki's six-meter carbon-fiber arm did not bend with gravity but stretched straight over the moss marsh and thoroughly illuminated the four chairs aligned beyond it.

Panasonic produced the Fukitorimushi ("wipe-up bug") using NANOFRONT. Exactly the size of a dust cloth, this flat robot wipes the floor by nimbly creeping along like an inchworm arching its back. In Japan, where we remove our shoes before entering the house, the ideal is a completely spotless floor. The sight of multiple lifelike robots, sensors blinking, crawling about on the venue's wooden floor, very like leeches, gave visitors in Milan a quiet but profound case of the shivers.

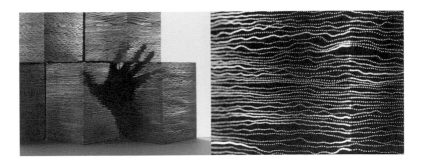

Kengo Kuma's Con/Fiber, concrete embedded with fiberoptic cables; material: ESKA

The architect Kengo Kuma used ESKA, a material in which countless optical fibers are embedded in concrete. He made a small pavilion out of isosceles triangle blocks, shaped like slices of cake, with the pointed ends facing inward. The triangles created a differential between the exterior and interior surface areas, amplifying the outside light by 1.8 times inside the pavilion. In buildings made of stone or brick, windows are opened in the walls to let in light, a concept that contrasts with Japanese shoji wood-framed paper sliding doors that provide indirect daylight. But concrete that allows light to enter offers translucence while retaining solidity. Removing boundaries like walls and windows gives rise to an enigmatic, ambiguous space. Kuma's piece was built on a small scale, but it revealed huge possibilities for architecture.

Nendo, a design company based in Tokyo, chose the non-woven, thermoplastic fiber SMASH to create a collection of lampshades. Covering deflated balloons with the fiber and then

Nendo's Blown Fabric; material: SMASH

inflating them in hot water – this method puffs the fibers into the exact shape of the balloons, as if they were made of blown glass. After they're taken out of the water, the balloons are deflated and removed, leaving fiber lampshades like shed skins, each unique in shape. Fitted with LEDs, they become lighting fixtures – seamless floating shapes exuding transmitted light, with the texture of organic fabric. A phalanx of more than one hundred appears like a colony of glowing mushrooms. With the light intensity regulated slowly with dimmers, they seem to inhale and exhale. It was a thrilling sight.

The iconic Italian product designer Antonio Citterio created a "sofa with gently rising supports" by using the multilayered stretch fabric FINEX, which is both pliable and durable. Citterio, who has designed the best-selling luxury sofa in the world, is intimately versed in the fundamentals of seating. This ovoid piece looks like a flat bed, but with the push of a button, two backrests rise in different directions from the center of the

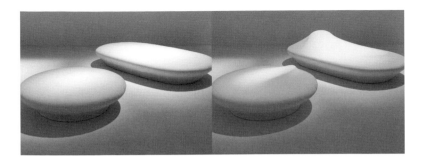

Antonio Citterio's Moshi-Moshi; material: FINEX

seating surface, converting it into a sofa, smoothly adjustable to any angle. I'm astounded and wonder why there's never been a sofa like this before.

Automaker Nissan allowed us to shrink their Cube into a quarter-scale "smiling car." The front of a car is a natural metaphor for the human face, and if its surface is made of pliable, durable stretch fabric, a car can "smile." While the honk of the

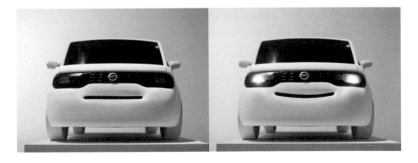

Nissan Motor Company, Ltd. Design Center + Hara Design Institute, NDC; material: ROICA

horn suggests a threat, a smiling expression would considerably soften the atmosphere of the streets. We commissioned a company specializing in animatronics – one that mechanically creates life-like expressions in Hollywood animals and aliens and such – and it developed the natural facial expressions for this piece. It's surprisingly difficult to create a smile that doesn't appear exaggerated, but thanks to this company's experience and wealth of precision technology, our car was able to smile naturally. There were a few incidents, including a temporary breakdown of the car's control device, which led to an awkward grin, but the exhibition ended with a record-breaking 38,000 visitors in its ten days.

TOKYO FIBER / SENSEWARE exhibition venue: Milano Triennale 2009

In the *SENSEWARE* exhibition, we did as many inter-
views as we could and netted more than two hundred instances
of media exposure. A number of detailed articles were written.
One comment that pleased me in particular was "At the least,
exhibitions are supposed to present the past, but in this one,
it's the future that is clearly on display." More than a few spoke
of it as "very Japanese." I hadn't introduced a single item sym-
bolizing Japanese tradition. But this was how the European
media reviewed our attempt at manifesting the future through
leading-edge technologies and materials. This critique from

overseas helped me sense what the world expects from Japan; that was the moment when, through advanced fibers, I arrived at a sense of possibilities for Japan's future.

Milano Triennale: The venue was designed as a white space because the exhibits were made of undyed fibers.

Chapter 6

Point of Growth: Design for a Future Society

After the Tohoku Earthquake

In the years to come, the disaster following the March 2011
Tohoku earthquake will be seen as a historic reference point. To
respond to this catastrophe, we need to cope with the enormous
destruction inflicted by the tsunami and the radioactive contamination. While fully aware that Japan is currently past its era of
growth and shrinking demographically, I would like to present a
way for us to deal with this situation by facing our future together.
My specialty is communication design, so my goal is to find a way
to respond to the flow of practical wisdom around the world concerning reconstruction, editing and utilizing it to see what kind of
motivation and vision can be called forth in response to a disaster
of this magnitude.

I visited towns on the Sanriku coast that were devastated
by the massive tsunami: Otsuchi, Kamaishi, Toni, Sanriku,
Ofunato, Rikuzentakada, and Kesennuma. This northeastern
region of Honshu has a rugged coastline eroded by the sea. It has
been hit by countless tsunamis over the centuries. Its natural
beauty pierces my heart. The same waves that formed this topography ravaged the cities built there.

Houses are no longer made of wood and straw; at some
point in the twentieth century, cities were rebuilt in steel and concrete. But even those cities were flattened by nature's fury. In
March 2011, debris stretched as far as the eye could see and was
quite difficult to clear away. Toppled and fragmented concrete
utility poles, the rebar stripped from within, reflected the fierce

destructive power of nature. The hulks of ships perched atop the wreckage of city streets evoked an indescribable sense of emptiness amid this devastated landscape.

Exposed to the atmosphere of the stricken area and after connecting with some of the local people, I came away with the firm belief that, rather than simply providing reconstruction assistance, it's essential to collaborate with them to develop a new future-oriented plan. I sensed that it would be important to have an image of a new vanguard of wisdom nurtured here, for the local people, the people of Japan, and people around the world.

Reconstruction includes short-term and long-term planning, but first we must give material and emotional support to the victims in their daily lives, and create work for them. As far as securing temporary housing is concerned, I heard from many sides that careful consideration must be given to communities and human relationships in temporary accommodations. In this respect, it seems that the experience of the Kobe Earthquake of 1995 has been put to good use.

The problem was how to plan the long-term reconstruction of these towns and industries. Even without this disaster, this region epitomized a Japan shrinking demographically through rural depopulation and an aging population. In most of the areas that lost population to the disaster, things are not likely to look up, even if recovery is achieved. If this were a time of rapid economic and population growth, the scars of the disaster would be gradually covered over by the natural expansion of these cities and towns. Of course it's important that a secure lifestyle be restored to people who are growing older, but that's not enough. A radical restructuring of these communities is being explored, one that might make municipal and harbor functions more efficient by consolidating several cities and ports.

The very first thing usually discussed after tsunami damage is rebuilding on higher ground and abandoning residences in low-lying areas. Lowlands are certainly susceptible to tsunamis, which is probably why there are towns and villages that adopt such plans. But this is probably not the only solution. There must be people at the cutting edge of architecture and civil engineering who can make proposals from a different perspective. In China and in Asia's other emerging nations, we see many examples of innovative urban planning proposals that draw on international expertise and overturn conventional wisdom. Now past the era of brick and concrete, we are entering a time in which we can create robust artificial infrastructure. We should be able to create a new city format with residences rising near seaports on gentle hills set back from scenic coastlines with temperate weather.

The most logical route to reconstruction might be to build a seawall that could protect the land from a midsized tsunami or typhoon. But if the budget were to be depleted paying for seawall construction, there would be little room left to think creatively about the future. It's said that it costs ¥100 million to build a meter of seawall. To build a seawall north to south along the affected area, only 130 kilometers long, would cost ¥13 trillion, spending the majority of the reconstruction budget on this single project. How about clearly differentiating between a structure that is predicated on being swept away by a large-scale tsunami every century and a more substantial, durable facility that can protect human life with certainty – and then combining the two? The Japanese people have a capacity for accepting impermanence. That's probably why we also need to be prepared to accept our fate when it is time to go. So I think it would be best not to encase the entire shoreline in concrete, but to let parts of it return to nature.

The ocean off the Sanriku coast is one of the richest fishing grounds in the world. It's quite possible to restore the fishing grounds and fish processing industries here. We should be able to raise the funds, both from Japan and from the rest of the world, to help the people and the industry of the area. The plains also present a great latent opportunity, not only as land for rice cultivation, but also for dairy and vegetable farming. If we can take advantage of this opportunity to work intensively on rethinking business operations, we may be able to draw up an ambitious plan for the future of farming in the region. We must build into the reconstruction plan the kind of appeal and hope for the area that will attract young people again.

However, there's a mentality at work that tends to cautiously promote reconstruction and to observe a respectful period of mourning after a great disaster, narrowing the possibilities and leading to plans that are realistic but rather stark. If I am urged to come up with a plan attuned to the DNA of local communities, it will make me want to avoid undue meddling. But that's something we should think about. Japan's bullet trains are amazing, but the stations and the atmosphere around them are so standard and commonplace that they induce relentless boredom. We should never build structures like this again. We should assemble the wisdom of Japan and the world to project a vision of the future that takes our spirits forward, a vision we could not create without this kind of opportunity.

Japan has no lack of architectural talent. Particularly at a time like this – in response to a national disaster – architects should be encouraged to fully apply their expertise. I also hope to see university research institutions and think tanks present reports from their distinctive research fields.

For instance, I think the "Orange Rounds" concept for mobile public facilities proposed by University of Tokyo professor Hidetoshi Ono, who premises his urban planning on the shrinking Japanese society, might be realized at this critical point. In this concept, vehicles designed as a medical clinic, a library, a movie theater, and a gym would circulate regularly among several towns. Because each vehicle is designed to be housed in a structure in each town, when the vehicle changes, the interior of the structure changes, and consequently, the facilities change as well. Where a clinic is parked today, there will be a movie theater tomorrow, and a library the next day. This is an idea for multiple adjacent towns to share various rotating services to control costs.

Environmental and energy researchers are refining proposals to promote a low-carbon, energy-efficient society, and manufacturers of high-tech products are accelerating the implementation of scenarios for new energy distribution systems based on storage battery technology. Even without specific requests from countries or municipalities, young designers are also beginning to voluntarily expand their activities.

This system, like a giant parabolic antenna, picking up an infinite number of products of grassroots wisdom, is perfectly suited to the grand design of reconstruction. It is not a top-down, centralized system, but one that prioritizes the reception of a diversity of ideas. We need to bring greater amounts of knowledge into the system. As ideas collide, they grow more precise – and can then be edited into easily understandable formats and sent through appropriate media to the people of the affected areas. The local people wouldn't have to accept all of these ideas, but it would dramatically increase their chances of being exposed to a variety of innovative ideas. After all, new ideas are hard to come by when we're wrapped up in our daily routines.

We have a variety of media, and of course the Internet, but in this case, I think books and magazines are the best option. After a disaster, what were people thinking and what kinds of proposals were made? For an accurate record of this, the print media, with their more stable information, good credibility, and ease of use, seem superior to the fluidity of the Internet. Magazines would stimulate debate and face-to-face interactions in the affected towns because people could read and discuss them over a bowl of noodles. An appropriate agency could take responsibility for editing and publication, and publish as many issues as the accumulation of ideas required. Of course the Internet could be utilized concurrently, playing the role of an information highway.

If the information could be shared among not only the victims, but also among people in other parts of Japan and the world, Tohoku would be seen as a place that fostered hope.

Whether or not specific reconstruction proposals are actually adopted is less important than the question of how to awaken people and lend them strength. Even if a certain plan isn't implemented, I think it's enough that local people get a sparkle in their eye from considering a fresh viewpoint. And ideas are not limited to areas that have experienced disasters – they can be used anywhere. If Tohoku can become a place from which lofty visions and possibilities for the future come streaming forth, then I'm sure it will have a bright future.

Nuclear accidents are still a matter that allows little room for error, but what I can do personally is to cooperate in spreading basic literacy about radiation. If we focus too closely now on the right or wrong of nuclear energy, there will be no refuge for the evacuees. Damage caused by misinformation is not just a problem for agriculture and the fishing industry. It's also a serious matter for Japan, which aims to be a tourist-oriented country. The flow of tourists to Japan fell after March 2011. Some countries even began to limit imports of Japanese industrial products. This situation won't improve unless we spread radiation literacy.

Japan can use this opportunity to transform itself into a leader in low energy consumption and renewable energy; we will probably have to reconsider nuclear energy within a new framework. In addition to safety concerns, nuclear energy involves the fundamental challenge of how to dispose of nuclear waste.

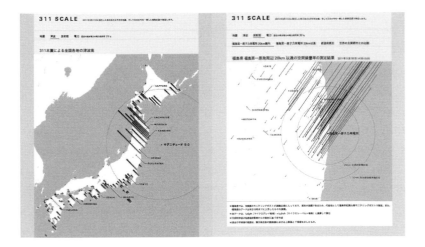

311 SCALE: An online project employing a coherent visual language to disseminate information regarding the March 2011 Tohoku earthquake and Japan's current status. Left: tsunami. Right: radiation.

Ultimately I favor switching to clean energy. However, before we do that, we must appeal to the world with a rational approach to dealing with the ongoing threat of radioactive material and radiation. We must begin again with precise measurement of radiation levels to ensure objectivity and credibility – an unavoidable responsibility for a country that has met with a nuclear disaster.

At the Nippon Design Center, where I work, young designers and copywriters have begun to play a leading role in graphically presenting data about earthquakes and radiation online by integrating visual languages such as color and form with guidelines such as "easy to understand," and "as accurately as possible." As a person who makes things and experiences, I have to be honest: the immensity of the destruction and pollution really got to me. For a while, I felt uninspired to make anything at all, and tended to feel depressed. But it is precisely times like this when we need to have the guts to face the situation head on, taking on what has to be dealt with, being careful with that which requires care, moving forward and thinking about the future. Throughout our long history, people have overcome huge difficulties without tiring or slacking off. We have to overcome this disaster in the same way.

Adult Principles

I am told that in today's Japan, there are more diapers produced for adults than for children. They say that in forty-five years, more than a quarter of the population will be over the age of sixty-five, which sounds bleak. Japan will be the first society in the world to face demographic decline. How calmly we can respond to this situation will determine this country's future.

Through all of recorded history, human beings have sought to increase the population. I doubt humans have ever experienced population decrease under normal circumstances, though declines in fertility have been caused by climate change, epidemics, and war. Human activity as elucidated by anthropologists like Claude Lévi-Strauss demonstrates behavioral patterns that are a constant hymn to the overflowing energy of life. Even traditional cultural patterns in which women are "given" to men to form stable family units can be seen as a concern for the prosperity of the society, that is, population growth recognized as a barometer of fertility.

Overall, the human population is still growing, but the majority of advanced countries are changing course, toward population decline. In advanced industrialized societies today, women seek to limit childbirth and raising children as factors restricting their own engagement in society. Even when they do have children, the trend toward having only one has gradually become more prevalent. This could be a huge turning point; the nature of our world may be changing.

In societies ruled by kings or despots, individual freedoms have been restricted, but people still multiplied. Even after major wars, in which conflicts between nations crushed the individual, the human population continued to increase. Hundreds of thousands of lives were destroyed in an instant with the dropping of the atomic bombs on Hiroshima and Nagasaki, and yet still people multiplied, and eventually the stricken cities overflowed with more people than they had before the war. Yet today, in what could be called a fleeting peace, the human population has begun to decrease. Is it because people have found a greater joy than is found in having children? Or is our instinct for survival putting the brakes on a population greater than the earth can bear?

In any case, Japan is leading this trend, currently transitioning into an aging society. In the 1920s, Japan's population was 60 million. By the early 2000s, it had more than doubled, to close to 130 million – but now it is shrinking, and in about the same amount of time it is projected to reach 60 million again, at the end of this century. What is happening today in Japan?

Perhaps what evolves in a mature civil society – that is, one structured so that there is no oppression by an absolute power or authority and individuals are free to live as they choose – is a sensitivity to quality and balance in dealing with objects and information. With the spread and permeation of mass media, pyramidal or centralized organizational structures have difficulty functioning; consequently, values and information come to be re-evaluated in an open environment in which countless intelligences can interact. The reason politics seems so problematic today is because politicians are not the only ones who have information; in most cases, ordinary people have access to the same level of information, and in some cases, may have identified a direction for problem solving through a network of collective intelligence before the politicians do. In other words, perhaps the audience of the drama, rather than waiting breathlessly for the next development in the scenario, is frustrated by scriptwriters who have not developed the storyline as expected.

Whether it's about radioactive contamination or the scandals surrounding match fixing in sumo wrestling, people clamor for information to be released. Underlying this is the commonly shared assumption that we'll be able to reach the optimum solution more quickly if we entrust the issue to the practice of disclosure and a shared chain of unlimited crowd-based intelligence than if we leave it to a select few to decide behind closed doors. The sense that cool collective intelligence – not overheated mass ignorance – is the most efficient way to reach a rational solution is less an ideology than a certain kind of sensibility that has begun to function within society.

In a society in which individual freedom is guaranteed and information is abundantly available, our sensitivity to issues of equality and balance has grown keen. Few support the extreme selflessness of a mother, who already works hard taking care of children and running a household, doing things like "staying up all night knitting mittens," as a popular Japanese song goes. Women aspire to a position in society and want to live wisely with no disadvantages. The declining birth rate is not due to the simplistic reasoning that it costs a lot of money to raise children. It is a phenomenon rooted in a society in which everyone has been promised the advantages of freedom.

Nonetheless, oppression of individuals still lurks behind this new common sense. I think that there is a unique kind of oppression embedded in a social consciousness that encourages a rational linkage between concepts of "liberation" and "common ownership." For instance, consider the problem of community. There have been a variety of attempts at creating new communities with free and open social environments, as opposed to communities involving mutual interference. But is there oppression in this rational, progressive approach to human relations? Absolutely.

Lately, I've been reading about shared houses and shared offices. In the former, bedrooms are private but residents share common facilities such as the kitchen and bathroom. In shared offices, people share the functions of an office (reception, for example) but maintain a separate workspace for each person. The value system at work here is part of the social consciousness that is related to equality and balance. We accept the existence of others in our homes or workplaces, from which we instinctively wish to bar strangers. What makes this possible is a fragile shared consciousness that can skillfully suppress the individual part of ourselves, the part that makes us different from others. Is this a perfectly horizontal solidarity, with no protruding bits? Thanks to this sense of common bonds, the kitchen and bathroom are neatly cleaned and managed, with the awareness that they will be used by others. Of course, you might call such relationships "refined." But this tacit communal morality feels mildly oppressive to me.

"Friend" is a beautiful word; no one would think of it as the fountainhead of oppression. However, in the course of events, a community with highly developed shared values can possess a certain invisible exclusivity. That is, becoming friends with some can turn into pressure not to have friendships with others. Bullying results not so much from being identified as the target of attack, but from not being "friended" – the negative consequence of everyone's quest for friends. I think this kind of instability lurks in the endgame of freedom.

Following the Tohoku earthquake, the United States launched an aid effort called Operation Tomodachi (Operation Friends), which was slightly eerie to me. Were those who showed up wearing badges emblazoned with the word *tomodachi* really *friends* of ours? We were of course deeply moved by the voluntary support and encouragement of the great number of countries and organizations who offered us aid. But in the end, I feel that going forward, the "delicacy of relationships" among both individuals and nations will become more important.

In certain states in the United States, LGBT people are rejecting ordinary nursing homes and insisting on their own dedicated facilities. In California, where gay marriage is legal (as it has been across the U.S. since 2015), it seems that disclosing personal information actually makes life easier. As a result of sharing this status, they are not persecuted and are able to enjoy a more comfortable, sophisticated environment for their old age than will non-LGBT individuals. Our sensitivity to openness and sharing will determine whether it will be easy or difficult to live in the societies of the future.

On the other hand, we needn't assume that an aging society is one full of weak and slow-moving old people. Certainly, there will be a greater proportion whose physical decline will necessitate nursing care, but we see quite a few people in their sixties and seventies who don't exhibit any decline in activity or abilities. The ¥1000 banknote carries the portrait of the Meiji-period novelist Natsume Soseki at the age of forty-five; from today's eyes, he looks like a gentleman of substance in his sixties. It's my personal impression that today's elderly look about 30 percent younger than their early twentieth-century counterparts.

A study of the behavior of ants found that a certain percentage work constantly and a certain percentage loaf around. I've forgotten the precise numbers, but the study shows that even if one collects only diligent ants or only lazy ants, in the resulting group the ratio between the two remains the same. I find this very interesting. Perhaps the same is true of human society: the proportion of people in any group with a capacity for participating actively in society may stay the same, regardless of the age breakdown. In short, if our definition of "active" is not based on age but on purchasing power, experience, discernment, and unconventionality, then new and different types of activities and markets may develop in the society to come. Active derives from the confidence associated with a mature personality, one independent of all of our conventional models assessing balance and equilibrium.

The View from Beijing

My solo exhibition opened at the Beijing Center for the Arts, a contemporary art space in the former American Consulate, a Western-style building located in an elegant city block called the Legation Quarter near Tiananmen Square. This modern exhibition venue has four floors – two above and two below ground – and is divided into a series of diverse spaces with a total area of more than two thousand square meters. We were able to create a beautifully varied exhibition flow. At first, the exhibition was slated to be held at the National Art Museum of China, which was built at the same time as the Great Hall of the People, but when I made a preliminary inspection of the Beijing Center for the Arts, a facility equivalent to the annex of the museum, I quickly decided to hold it there, because a clear image came to me of the exhibition in this space.

For some time, I'd dreamed of opening an exhibition of significant scale in China because Asia's future is concentrated there. China's population is more than ten times that of Japan. This means there are ten times more spirited, courageous young people in China than in Japan. Pinning their hopes on the future of their country, they are studying all over the world, excelling in leading-edge science, technology, economics, business, architecture, and design, bursting with aspirations and desire and with the wind of their country's economic progress at their back. After a few years of gathering experience outside China, they return to their homeland and begin to work. Year after year, tens of thousands return to China. They speak foreign languages proficiently, and are skilled in the use of the latest technology. They also take a dispassionate attitude toward the world and business. These are the people leading China's business and culture.

This doesn't mean I want to follow China's example. Nor do I have some naive notion of using an exhibition to assert the superiority of Japanese design and break into the Chinese market. Precisely because China has been exposed continuously to the impact of globalization, the Chinese people must awaken to the possibilities of Asian culture and re-examine their own path. They must recognize anew that their resources lie not in the wisdom of the West, but in that of the East. It's likely that the more experience one gains in foreign countries, the easier it is to awaken to this self-realization and better understand the value of our own unique cultures. I would like to share this insight with the Chinese people.

Front Gate 23, the former American Consulate site near Tiananmen Square, was renovated into a venue for exhibiting modern art, the Beijing Center for the Arts.

We learned design from the West. At the same time that the West was discovering the shape of modern civilization, including the establishment of democratic states and the Industrial Revolution, it was putting rationality to work in the environment for human life, and creating the concepts of design and simplicity. The West was slightly ahead of the game in the progress of science and technology and the maturity of ideas for shaping the external physical environment.

Although Japan has a history going back over a thousand years, the Meiji Restoration of 1868 occasioned a wholesale importation of Western civilization. This was a setback in terms of cultural history, but it also enabled Japan to establish its standing as a modern state without being encroached upon by the Western powers. And after our defeat in World War II, Japan

Second floor of the Beijing Center for the Arts, the venue for *Designing Design*, Kenya Hara's 2011 solo exhibition.

was able to discover a pathway to economic survival via its startling breakthrough as an industrial nation. Nonetheless, along with the increasing abundance of things in our homes and opportunities for overseas travel, there is a growing trend toward recognizing the sensibilities of our own country. We left Japan behind in the Meiji era, and polluted our environment with industrialization, but we can't let our country end this way. A culture that we have upheld for more than a millennium is not something to be thrown away so easily, nor completely forgotten.

Beauty and pride may be found in all Japanese culture, not only in Katsura Rikyu, whose perfect architecture moved architect Bruno Taut to tears. The shape of *fusuma* sliding panels and shoji screens came into existence in response not only to the order of the space, but also to that of the body – that is, the

MUJI Art Direction section of the exhibition, accessed through the atrium of the first-floor entrance.

disciplined posture needed to open and close them. Japanese traditional architecture is coupled with the spirituality of how beautifully, and with what modest dignity, one faces the world and runs a home. In this book I've touched many times on the concept of applying this aesthetic sense to the shape of homes of the future, and to forms of tourism and hospitality.

The more economies globalize and the more interconnected structures of financing, investment, manufacturing, and distribution become, the more we long for cultural individuality. The world's cultures abhor the idea of being melded into a uniform, inorganic shade of gray. This abhorrence is rooted in the same sense of values celebrated by the World Heritage Sites. Happiness and pride occupy a different dimension than money does. The originality of one's own country's culture and the work

Chinese technicians constructed elaborate features for the exhibition at the Beijing Center for the Arts.

of polishing it with an eye to the future result in a sense of well-being and satisfaction.

When you view Japan from a place like Singapore, you get the feeling of looking from the home of a nouveau riche entrepreneur toward the mansion of the aristocratic Reizei family, with its tradition of *waka* poetry, a family that for eight centuries, under imperial order, secretly saved an important trove of documents that epitomized the culture of the ancient imperial court. Singapore is a place with a great view from which you can look out over the rest of Asia and the Pacific Rim with a cool attitude, from the Middle East to India, Southeast Asia, China, Taiwan, Korea, Japan, and Australia. This is why it is developing as a financial center, with a concentration of great riches. Yet its history is only forty-some years long. More than

seventy-five percent of the population is Chinese, but the dialects – Cantonese, Fujianese, Hakka, and so forth – have strong idiosyncrasies, so there are four official languages: English, Standard Chinese, Malaysian, and Tamil. There is wealth, but as for traditional culture, it's just the beginning. Traditions that have been handed down and protected for a millennium and more within a single culture have a unique luster when seen from a place like this.

Today, confronted by an era of slow growth, Japan is finally beginning to recognize its own history and traditions as a rare "soft" resource for creating value in a global context. And thanks to the activity of all of Asia, it is beginning to really feel the possibilities of a new cultural frontier taking shape in a world that has been dominated by the influence of Western civilization. Only through our unique experience of Westernization during the Meiji era and rapid postwar economic growth have we become

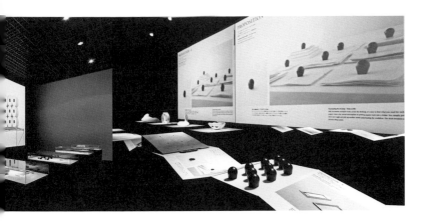

In the second basement level, the venue for *"Exhibiting Exhibitions"* was given a sense of realism by using projectors to represent the revivals of five exhibitions.

able to look at the world and our own culture with relative clarity. I would like to turn those experiences into a message and share it with today's Asia. It's high time we explore the path that will promote full recognition of both the economic and cultural potential of our own countries.

In my earlier book, *Designing Design* (2003), I touched on this potential for Asian culture. The book was translated into a relatively large number of languages, including Chinese (both simplified and traditional), Korean, and English, and, contrary to expectations, it gained many readers in China. In this book, I make the claim that the concept of design is not a tool to instigate consumption or a part of brand management know-how, but rather a means by which to awaken to the essence of everyday living and cultural pride. I was encouraged by the broadly positive response to this statement among readers, a reaction that motivated me to design an exhibition for Beijing.

The exhibition was organized by floor into three sections. The first floor was devoted to "Aspects of Design," exhibiting in detail facets of my own work, including corporate and brand identity, product design, space design, poster and book design, and so forth. It includes nostalgic pieces like early experimental posters, the opening and closing ceremony pamphlets for the Nagano Olympics, and early art direction for the Aichi Expo. Although to differing degrees, each of these pieces has a consciousness of Japan at its creative root.

On the second floor were examples of art direction for MUJI, for which I've served as art director and also an advisory board member since 2002. I introduce them to illustrate the value that a philosophy of craftsmanship backed by Japan's unique aesthetic can provide to the world: that simplicity can sometimes surpass luxury and splendor. Without displaying a single product, the point was to convey how ideas are assimilated and expressed by highlighting communication design – from the system of store tags and labels to posters and newspaper and magazine advertising.

The third level was a condensation, reorganization, and revival of the five exhibitions that I have curated. Through these, under the titles *RE DESIGN, HAPTIC, SENSEWARE*, and so on, I visualized and exhibited the importance of looking at daily life, and the five senses, as well as the possibilities for new fields of manufacturing and creation. Design plays a significant role in using exhibitions to make visible what is dormant or latent.

It took three years to realize this exhibition, but thanks to the enthusiasm of the director of the BCA, Ms. Weng Ling, and Zhu E, the art director of the National Art Museum of China, I was able to achieve an exhibition space with the precision and accuracy I was seeking. Thanks to the sponsorship of the Chinese People's Association for Friendship with Foreign Countries, we were able to share it with many people, both in the world of design and beyond.

At the banquet following the reception, mingling with those involved in government and education were old friends in the design world from Hong Kong, Shenzhen, and Guangzhou. And from Japan, the president of Musashino Art University, Yoji Koda, attended, as well as many others with whom I had worked over the years; I was quite teary-eyed that evening.

The exhibition venue bustled with visitors day after day. I also delivered lectures at Tsinghua University, China Central Academy of Fine Arts (CAFA), and the Beijing Design Walk venue, and was met in each by large, enthusiastic audiences. At one university, twice we had to move to a larger facility. Even so, the students were packed in, right up to the stage. I sensed a huge response to the call to re-examine Asia's culture. It made me feel as if I were in direct contact with the birth of the culture of the future.

A collaborative project fusing tradition and the future is already underway. A new design project is stirring in Jingdezhen, the area that produces a porcelain that boasts the highest degree of perfection as one of China's traditional crafts, and in a Chan

(Zen) temple built during the Sui dynasty (589–618) in Xiangyang, an old town in the middle of the Yangtze River basin.

The exhibition toured to Shanghai and Qinhuangdao, on the Bohai Sea. This was the beginning of my journey interacting deeply and broadly with Asia's people, as well as reconsidering the future of my own design – looking for a form in which I could use all of my strength to throw something as far as I can.

The exhibition's entrance,
with books arrayed on display stands.

Postscript

This book is an edited collection of articles originally written for the magazine *Tosho*, for a column called "The Education of Desire." They were written over a two-year period beginning in September 2009. I didn't think I was up to the task of a column, but once I started, strangely enough, it became part of the rhythm of my life.

Because it is the designer's role to take up only the trivial and troublesome matters of the world, his daily work is as restless as the acrobatics of a juggler with many balls in the air. He holds only two in his hands at any given moment – but who knows how many balls are in the air?

Once I started counting my projects, but I became queasy and stopped. The word "busy" is taboo. Once the work I toss high in the air disappears beyond the clouds, it's best to forget that it will soon return. That way, when it does land back in my hands, it feels fresh.

Writing for a magazine is something done in the midst of that juggling. If I were to describe the scene, it's as if I were both making and juggling rice balls at the same time. I kept the ones I'd made going without dropping them and molded new ones as I went, adding them to those in the air. A ball or two may have accidentally gotten a grain of rice stuck to the seaweed wrap, or the shape might have been a bit off, but somehow, without dropping any, I managed to finish twenty-four rice balls.

As a result, these have now been packed into the bento

box known as the Iwanami Shinsho paperback series and sent out into the world. "The Education of Desire" was not considered a strong title. Initially, Yoshiko Furukawa suggested I title it *Dezain Rikkoku* (A Nation by Design). Looking at that little row of misshapen rice balls, I was taken aback by the publisher's creativity in coming up with such an impressive title. True, I wrote about a future vision for the country, so *A Nation by Design* or *Japan by Design* would be far clearer than the roundabout *The Education of Desire*. However, I began to feel uneasy about this title.

In the end, the straightforward title *Designing Japan* became the name of the single bamboo-leaf wrapper enclosing these twenty-four rice balls. The subtitle *A Future Built on Aesthetics* indicates that it's not about Japan's traditional culture. In my publishing experience so far, the more serious the book, the less likely my proposed title would be accepted; they all end up reflecting advice from the editors. For my previous monograph, *Designing Design*, I came up with the title *Why Design?*, but the editor wanted me to make it a more imposing title, asserting, "*This* is design!"

Designing Japan is a companion to *Designing Design*, but it is also like a flowchart of my work for the near future. I think I will walk along for some time to come carrying this map. I wonder what you'll think of these irregular rice balls. They are stuffed with the usual – pickled plum, kelp, or salmon caviar, with a morsel of sweet omelet on the side. If there is anything I've missed or done wrong, please let me know.

Masanori Sakamoto, of the editorial department of

Iwanami Shoten: I am grateful for your continuing encouragement. Thanks to you, I was able to organize my thoughts and transform these articles into a book. Takeko Tomita, editor-in-chief of *Tosho*, whose prompt monthly edits allowed me to continue writing with peace of mind: with your great support, I was able to finish this two-year project. And Yoshiko Furukawa of Iwanami Shinsho, who first awakened me with the punchy title *A Nation by Design* and continually smacked the rump of this sluggish ox toward publication: it is thanks to you that I was able to put one foot in front of the other.

I would also like to use this opportunity to express my deep gratitude to every individual at Nippon Design Center's Hara Design Institute, each of whom lives in the universe of our endless endeavors. It is thanks to being able to work with all of you that I am able to constantly move forward in the realm of thought. In particular, I want to express my gratitude for their faithful service in our publication projects to Yukie Inoue, who generously tolerates the mismanagement of her imperfect boss, and Kaoru Matsuno, who always offers her devoted and accurate attention to the very end.

Finally, I give praise and appreciation to my dear wife. *Tosho* is the only magazine she has subscribed to for nearly thirty years, and it was a secret source of encouragement to me as an author to know that she would be reading my words in its pages.

Photo Credits

Page 13   *Dream Design* 11 (Magazine House, 2003)

Pages 19, 21, 23, 25 Design Platform Japan Special Edition, conceived and edited
                      by Shigeru Ban and Kenya Hara,
                      JAPAN CAR: Designs for the Crowded Globe (Asahi Shuppan, 2009)

Page 27   Above: Photo: Taisuke Yoshida
                      Below: Photo: Shinji Hattori (Studio Big)

Page 29   *JAPAN CAR: Designs for the Crowded Globe.*
                      Production: Hitachi Corporation

Page 45   Left and Above Right: Gabriele Fahr-Becker ed., *The Art of East Asia*
                      (Konemann, 1999). ©Rheinisches Bildarchive, Cologne
                      Right: *The Art of East Asia.* ©Dr. G. Gerster /
                      Agentur Anne Hamann, Munich

Page 49   Left: Florence de Dampierre, supervised by Kageyu Noro, Shunji Yamada,
                      Chairs: A History (Toyo Shorin, 2009) Collection: I. Goldsmith, Christie's
                      Right: *Marcel Breuer Design* (Taschen, 2001).
                      Designsammlung Ludewig, Berlin. Photo: Lepkowski

Page 56   Photo: Yoshihiko Ueda

Page 95   Above: Kenzo Tange and Walter Gropius, *Katsura: Tradition and Creation
                      in Japanese Architecture* (Zokeisha, 1960). Photo: Yasuhiro Ishimoto
                      Below: Yasuhiro Ishimoto, *Katsura Rikyu* (Rikuyosha, 2010)

Page 130   Production: Nippon Design Center

Pages 151–60   Product photos: Voile. Venue photos: Nacasa & Partners

Page 171   Production: Nippon Design Center

Pages 180–85   Photos: Nacasa & Partners

                      Uncredited photos and drawings are the author's.

About the Author

Kenya Hara (b. 1958) is an internationally acclaimed graphic designer and professor at Musashino Art University in Tokyo. He has been MUJI's Art Director since 2002. Hara creates design that elicits experiences, as well as designing objects. He developed *RE DESIGN: Daily Products of the 21st Century*, an exhibition that re-examined the meaning of the word "design." *RE DESIGN* toured internationally, receiving both the Icograda Excellence Award and the Icsid Design Excellence Award at the 17th Biennial of Industrial Design and the Mainichi Design Award 2000. Hara went on to develop and tour *HAPTIC: Awakening the Senses* and *SENSEWARE*, through which he advocated for keywords that update existing value systems. He developed designs deeply rooted in Japanese culture for the opening and closing ceremonies of the 1998 Nagano Winter Olympics, and for the promotion of Expo 2005, held in Aichi prefecture. Hara handled product design for such corporations and designers as the beverage company AGF and KENZO, and visual identity campaigns for the renewal of the Matsuya Ginza department store, the MORI Building, the bookstore Tsutaya Shoten, and GINZA SIX. Since 2015 he has been the General Producer of the JAPAN HOUSE project, an initiative of the Ministry of Foreign Affairs. Hara is the recipient of the Tokyo Art Directors Club Grand Prize (2003) for his MUJI advertising campaign, the Kodansha Publishing Culture Award, and the Japan Inter Design Forum Prize, among others. His book *Dezain no Dezain* (Iwanami Shoten, 2003) received the Suntory Prize for Social Sciences and Humanities. After being translated into Chinese, Korean, and Taiwanese, it was expanded and published in English as *Designing Design* (Lars Müller Publishers, 2007), gaining a broad international readership. Hara's other books include *White* (Lars Müller Publishers, 2009) and *Architecture for Dogs* (TOTO Shuppan, 2013).

About the Translators

Maggie Kinser Hohle and Yukiko Naito are partners in Takumi Translation, which aims to broaden global understanding by conveying the achievements and perspectives of creative masters. They have translated most of Kenya Hara's books and catalogues into English, including *Designing Design* and *HAPTIC: Awakening the Senses*. They also translated Leonard Koren's classic, *Wabi-Sabi for Artists, Designers, Poets & Philosophers*, from English to Japanese. Based in Nagoya, Naito has a background in Zen Buddhism and has translated a number of Buddhist books. Based in northern California, Hohle is a nonfiction writer educated in philosophy who worked in Japan for fifteen years.

（英文版）日本のデザイン―美意識がつくる未来
Designing Japan: A Future Built on Aesthetics

2018年3月27日　第1刷発行

著　者　原　研哉
訳　者　マギー・キンザー・ホーリ
　　　　内藤ゆき子
発行所　一般財団法人出版文化産業振興財団
　　　　〒101-0051 東京都千代田区神田神保町3-12-3
　　　　電話　03-5211-7282（代）
　　　　ホームページ　http://www.jpic.or.jp/

印刷・製本所　株式会社サンエムカラー